MAY 23   4912

614-569-4912

ANTIQUE AND
MODERN
TEDDY BEARS

pg 77   Dicky

THE OFFICIAL® PRICE GUIDE TO

ANTIQUE AND MODERN TEDDY BEARS

Kim Brewer
and
Carol-Lynn Rössel Waugh

FIRST EDITION

HOUSE OF COLLECTIBLES · NEW YORK

©1988 Random House, Inc.

This is a registered trademark of Random House, Inc.

All rights reserved under International and
Pan-American Copyright Conventions.

Published by: The House of Collectibles
201 East 50th Street
New York, New York 10022

Distributed by Ballantine Books, a division of Random House, Inc., New York, and simultaneously in Canada by Random House of Canada Limited, Toronto.

Manufactured in the United States of America

ISBN: 0-876-37792-4

First Edition: April 1990

10 9 8 7 6 5 4 3 2

This book is dedicated to
DOROTHY AYERS,

whose imagination, stamina, and
endless patience have helped to bring
about the American Teddy Bear Revolution.
To many of us she will always be
"Queen of the Bruins."

K. B.

This book is dedicated in loving memory to Carl Frederick Leopold Rössel (January 7, 1909–September 6, 1989), who passed away just as it was completed. I miss you, Daddy, and treasure the time we had together.

Carol-Lynn Rössel Waugh

Table of Contents

APPENDIXES

Foreword

A KEY TO TREASURE

By Beverly Matteson Port . . . Artist, Collector, and Lecturer. Beverly is America's premier teddy bear artist and has long been recognized among bear designers and collectors as a moving force in the current teddy bear popularity explosion. She pioneered the teddy bear as an art form, coining the phrase "The American Teddy Bear Artist" and is known as the leader in her field. She is said to be the person most responsible for the current interest in teddy bears today. She has been the inspiration and role model for thousands of artists and collectors the world over. Beverly has collected antique dolls, toys, and teddy bears for over thirty years.

❦

You have just opened a valuable book and hold a key to treasure in your hands! A key to treasure from the past, the present, and in the future. A key to years of enjoyment as well as investment possibilities. Learn from this book. Study it and keep it by your side in your travels, for one never knows when its knowledge will be needed. It will unlock the door to discoveries in a field long unrecognized by others until I was the first to champion its cause among collectors many years ago. A world of sharing and friendship awaits you in one of the fastest-growing collecting fields today: antique and modern teddy bears.

In the 1950s and 1960s—when, as a student and then a professional artist, I found this key to a fascinating field—it was not only ignored as a separate collecting category but looked down on. I had been incorporating the teddy bear, along with the doll, in my drawings and other art projects, including stained-glass window design; but when I began creating original soft-sculpture teddy bears from old mohair and alpaca coats, even my art colleagues looked askance at me. Still I continued to create my "Raggedi-baer Family" and "Bears of Olde," along with other multimedia art forms. Then, when they found out that I was also a collector of those "dirty old things"—old teddy bears and fabric dolls—I heard laughter! No one is laughing now! Today those fragile antique-textile "friends of childhood" are bringing hundreds and thousands of dollars at auctions, sales, and conventions the world over, from the many collectors now involved in the antique bear field. The artist bear field, also established by my early efforts, is a main source of support for many artists and craftspeople today and has influenced the present commercial area. This field, although still rela-tively new compared to antiques, is growing with explosive speed.

The teddy bear, first created in the early 1900s, gained popularity that grew rapidly to fad proportions, with adults as well as children coming under his spell. One favorite advertisement from the early 1900s was titled "Teddy Bears Are All the Rage"; and rage it was—a craze that grew, with 1907 termed "The Year of the Bear." The early wild years calmed down, the bear changed in form during the ensuing decades, appearing in many styles. He later became absorbed into the whole toy field. By the 1950s and 1960s fewer and fewer companies made jointed bears.

The variety of bears was at a low ebb in the late 1950s and early 1960s when I searched for them for my first child. When my daughter was tiny, the movement of the teddy bear's jointed limbs and head were what fas-cinated her the most. As an artist, I had already begun making jointed teddy bears along with other soft-sculpture works; not as toys, like those dolls and bears I had made in the beginning, when I was ten or so years old, for my baby sisters. Some teddy bears I created for those astute pa-trons interested in them as soft-sculpture art forms.

The antique teddy bears were being discarded and destroyed when I began collecting and creating. I was intrigued by the histories of the old well-loved toys, entreating people not to throw them away, for I believed in their importance to the future. When, in the 1950s, I paid a dollar for an old 12-inch 1905 Steiff, it was greeted with the same disbelief as if I'd purchased a stray kitten when everyone was giving them away free!

In the early 1960s the World's Fair opened in Seattle. The German Import store was a favorite stop on my visits. There, packed in dozens to each original box, like little sausages, were little Schuco teddy bears from Germany. They were 2 1/2 and 3 1/2 inches tall, selling for $1.25 and $1.50 each and in many, many different colors. I purchases several of each color.

Why didn't I buy whole boxes of them? Because they were plentiful; they were considered children's toys. Why was an adult more interested in them than her two-year-old daughter was? Were there strange stares when faces were compared for the "right look" before the purchase? Yes, many stares! In fact, the comments of salespeople were designed to embarrass, not encourage. Still, during each visit to the World's Fair, the store was checked to see if new colors of the tiny jointed bears had arrived, and a few more were purchased. Gradually, over the next six years, their prices rose to $4.50, then to $8 and $12; that's when I stopped buying. They disappeared from stores entirely. In the late 1970s I saw them at collectors' shows for $25 to $30. By then my articles, slide programs, lectures, and seminars for collectors on the subject of teddy bears—their creation, histories, repair, and restoration—had taken effect. Now the "little darlings" command prices up to a hundred times the original prices—and more, depending on the rarity of color.

In 1961 there was a toy sale in a department store in Portland, Oregon. A 31-inch Steiff teddy was purchased for $21, half his original price, but his 25-inch "smaller brother," priced at $15, was left behind. A short time later they were discontinued. In the early 1980s another "smaller brother" appeared at an antique show. His price was $500. Last year bears identical to him were offered at $1,500 to $1,800. The 3 1/2-inch jointed Steiff bears, purchased for $2 and $2.50 for my toddler daughter's and baby son's little hands to hold, were discontinued by the mid-1960s. The only small ones available were not jointed but had bendable arms and legs with wire armatures inside. The joints in the small early Steiff bears became a sought-after feature, and they now are $300 and up.

In the mid-1970s, while getting ready to attend the UFDC National Convention in Wisconsin, with a certain amount of money saved for purchases there, a hard decision came along. Just before I left Washington State, a pair of 14-inch white Steiff teddy bears were offered for $50, and I hesitated—there were no price guides then. There was no informational material nor books in the teddy bear collecting field to indicate future trends and values, only the "comparative research" articles, columns, and programs I was doing to heighten interest and bring the information to the attention of other people. The hesitation was brief, however. The purchase was completed and has never been regretted, for bears at the national convention were not plentiful and were $35 to $50 each. And an article by me in the 1975 National Convention book probably had helped call attention to their price-worthiness.

In 1978 I passed up an early 14-inch German Yes/No Schuco teddy bear in mint condition for about $100. I thought it was too high, but regretted my decision a short time later. Vintage American and English bears were left on sales tables as well, to later regret. Though many more people were now interested in the teddy bear field because of the positive response to my programs, lectures, and articles, there was still nothing to guide me or help in my decisions. Ah yes, you say, that wasn't very long ago. No, it wasn't long ago—only 12 to 15 years! Look through this book and find today's price for similar bears. Oh, you just did! Now you see why I refer to this book as not only a guide but a key to treasure! All I had was my intuition and love for bears.

Each time prices rise, there is a tendency to think they won't go higher; and indeed they do level off in some cases for a short time—before they begin to rise again. The same case can be made for some artist bears. A case in point: In the late 1970s the preordered original teddy bears copyrighted as the "Time Machine Teddies" were exhibited at shows in the 1970s. Many people not "into" bears would go past and say, "Ninety-five dollars for an artist-created teddy bear? It will never catch on! It's only because you have become so identified with teddy bears. Others won't be able to do it! You are an exception!" Now, dear reader, please scan the price ranges in the artist section. Indeed, it did "catch on." Later, in 1981, one of the "Time Machine Teddies" was awarded "Best of Show" from among 150 handmade bears, in a week-long show at Teddy 'N Friends in Minnesota that was attended by 17,000 people. Today there are hundreds of bearmakers and thousands of handmade bears.

My sculpted bears and other animals, including cats and rabbits—some "mixed media" with porcelain heads or faces—were winning Best of Class ribbons and many other awards, along with my artist dolls in the 1970s, inspiring other artists to begin creating in the field. I was guest editor for a complete teddy bear issue of the United Federation of Doll Clubs' *Doll News* magazine, Winter 1976, and photographed a scene with my daughter's artist teddy bears for the cover. My antique and originally created bears, as well as my son's, were also in this issue. It is a "landmark issue," for interest boomed among collectors! My Puss in Boots graced the *Doll News* cover in 1979, as well as several other magazines. The interest in artist-created animals continued its rapid climb. As a result of this increased interest, two national magazines asked me to begin writing regular monthly articles on teddy bears and other animal dolls in 1976. Many people now well known in the field have said that they read and were tremendously inspired by those early articles, the only thing "going" for teddy bears at that time.

I also wrote articles about other artists who were beginning to make teddy bears in that period and coined the term "American Teddy Bear Artist." My magazine columns were titled "Theodore B. Bear Says"— Theodore is an artistic creation of mine. Fourteen years later, he is still my co-author for my "Let's Talk Teddy Bears" column in *Teddy Bear and Friends* collectors' magazine. Among other authors writing in the field now are my son, John Port: "The Bear Sleuth" column; and my daughter, Kimberlee Port: "Kimberlee's Kitchen" column for the *Teddy Bear Review* magazine.

The antique bear and the art bear—two important fields in the teddy bear world so loved and championed by Theodore B. Bear and myself— are brought together in this book you hold in your hands. There are parallels and there are differences. The antique bears were made by companies primarily as toy objects—time and quality giving them value and making them collectibles. Artistic flair shows in many, from the individual designers and workers who put them together many years ago. The art bears are made today, primarily as collectibles, not toys; and again quality plays an important part. Certainly, artistic flair, originality, and innovation must be apparent in an art bear. In both types, appeal plays a big part in their collectibility, and certainly scarcity of type—especially "one-of-a-kinds"—adds greatly to their value to the collector. Some collectors look for a "name" bear; others collect by size, material, or country. There are a myriad of different reasons. I look for "heart and soul," and if the bear "looks" back at me, that's it! Home the teddy bear comes!

Antique museums house venerable specimens, and art galleries have opened their doors to the artist bear. Two of my art bears sold for record-breaking prices during the first professional art exhibit of American teddy bear artists at the Incorporated Gallery on Madison Avenue in New York in 1987, and they were responsible for establishing prices relative to other fine art objects.

The Golden Teddy awards were instituted by the *Teddy Bear Review* magazine in 1987, and my original art bears, as well as my commercially designed bears, were among those receiving the award medallions—and again in 1988 and 1989. In 1989 Kimberlee Port, also a Golden Teddy Award winner, introduced bears as an art form within the University of Washington's art school. Her innovative group of teddy bears will earn academic credits toward an art degree.

We who create, collect, and love the teddy bear believe his journey has only just begun. We look forward to more exciting events in the future.

The general public, not yet aware of this fabulous collecting field, continues to be unaware of the old bears' value. They relate to me, at large shows, the sad tales of bears given away, burned, or trashed "just yesterday." Family-owned and worn bears are records of loving hearts. They are as much a part of treasured family history as china, jewelry, or silver.

The art bear—an art form due greater and greater recognition and value in the future—has already come into its own in the present. And through this guide, even more people will become aware of this fascinating field.

Use this key to the treasure and pleasure in both the antique and artist bear fields—knowledge! This book will aid you in identification, values, and—most of all—information to help in making a personal collecting decision. Prepare for adventure—happy teddy bear hunting!

Beverly Matteson Port

Acknowledgments

Super-special thanks are due to the following: Nancy Torode and Patricia Volpe, for their extraordinary efforts; Lynn Trusdell and Gian Luiso for their photographic contributions; Paul Fellows, for his immense generosity; Barbara Lauver, for information retrieval and up-to-date news; Grace Dyar, for her insights into the adult toy collector; Billy and Betsy Bixby, Louise Laskey, Regina Brock, Marcia Sanderson, Sue Foskey, Kimberlee Port, and John Paul Port, for their energetic enthusiasm and support in photography and literary compilation; Susan Aller, for her impressive additions; Henry Kurtz, Bunny Campione, Olivia Bristol, and Dana Hawkes, for time taken from their busy schedules; Col. Thomas and May Carhart, Janet Finney, Michael Haller, The "Owl and the Pussycat," Dorothy Harris, Editor-in-Chief, House of Collectibles, Barbara Goldstein, Philip Scharper, Cindy Berman, Barbara Baldwin, Cohen Auctions, Theriault's Auctions, Sandra Kessler, Charles and Donna Jordan, David Douglas, Steve Schutt, Bob Holtz, Ingrid Wusstner, Sara Phillips, Doris Johnson, Kerry and Chester A. Curtis, and Arthur Senopole; Gigi, for her input; Charles Finney of Data Word, Simsbury, Connecticut, for his extravagant guidance and humor; and a very special thank you to technical consultant Beverly Matteson Port, for all her help with this book.

We'd like to thank Philip Draggan for creating the illustrations that appear in this book.

We also wish to thank the bearmakers who generously shared their bears, information, and photographs, and our families for their patience and forbearance with this project.

Prologue

HOW THE TEDDY BEAR GOT HIS NAME

Gregory C. Wilson is a former curator and head of the Theodore Roosevelt archive at Harvard University, the official presidential library. As he cataloged and upgraded the information files, he became fascinated with the president's bear-hunting trip to Mississippi and the story behind it. Later, while working at the Five College Library in Massachusetts, he was able to continue his research by reviewing the microfilmed collection of Theodore Roosevelt's documents and statements.

From the information Mr. Wilson has had access to over the years, he has formulated a new interpretation of the now famous cartoon "Drawing the Line."

Who made the first bear actually called a "teddy bear"? And what is the story behind it?

Gregory C. Wilson, a former curator and head of the Theodore Roosevelt archives at Harvard University confirmed what many people know: that the teddy bear has something to do with President Theodore Roosevelt. But Wilson brings a unique understanding to the story.

In November 1902, President Roosevelt was invited by Southern friends to go bear hunting in Mississippi. The president was in trouble with some Southern Republicans and National Republicans for his sponsorship of progressive social programs. He had further antagonized them by inviting Booker T. Washington to dine at the White House with his family and to advise him on the appointment of blacks to federal posts in the South. There was a move among Republicans to dump Roosevelt as their candidate in 1904 in favor of Senator Mark Hanna. Ever the politician, Roosevelt decided that he could consolidate his supporters in the South by appearing among them in the relaxed atmosphere of a hunting party, knowing well that the press would be following every aspect of the trip.

On the second day of the hunt the pack of hounds struck the trail of a bear, and the hunting party gave chase. After several hours of pursuit and waiting for the quarry to emerge from the dense brush, the president returned to camp. When the bear was finally cornered by the hounds, it was captured and tied to a tree and the president was summoned. When Roosevelt saw the animal, he refused to shoot it in such an unsportsmanlike way and ordered the bear put out of its misery. The bear weighed 235 pounds.

News of the day's events quickly reached the papers. Two days later, on November 16, 1902, a cartoon montage was published on the front page of *The Washington Star*. It was drawn by the *Post*'s political cartoonist, Clifford K. Berryman, and comprised five separate cartoons, one of which showed the president refusing to shoot an unhappy bear cub tied by a rope around its neck. The caption read: "Drawing the line in Mississippi."

Gregory Wilson suggests that the caption referred to the "color line" and was a political commentary that would have been clearly understood by readers in 1902. It is saying that Roosevelt was unyielding in his support for black civil rights at a time when these were being denied in many Southern states. "The cartoon was not," Wilson asserts, "a commentary on Roosevelt as a conservationist, or, as some maintain, a reference to any boundary dispute in Mississippi that the president had been asked to adjudicate."

The public was enchanted by the little bear and wanted more of it. Berryman obliged and soon was drawing a bear in every cartoon in which the president appeared. Often the bear carried a motto or spoke. "Teddy's Bear" became Berryman's trademark.

It was not long before stuffed toy bears called "Teddy's Bear" began to appear, in response to an obvious market opportunity. One of the first was made by Morris Michtom, a Brooklyn candy store owner, and his wife. It was displayed in the window of their shop with a price tag of $1.50. Michtom's grandchildren tell the story of how Michtom wrote to the president, asking for permission to use the name "Teddy's Bear" for his toy and of Roosevelt's reply that it was all right with him but that he didn't see how it would help the bear business! Little did Roosevelt—or Michtom—guess that the teddy bear would propel Michtom and his family into big business in the form of the Ideal Toy Company, which used as its motto "Excellence in Toy Making Since the Teddy Bear."

At the same time, the Steiff jointed bear was transformed through the mysteries of marketing into "Teddy's Bear," and by the end of 1904 Steiff had sold 12,000 of them. This number increased to nearly a million by 1907, when it was finally known as the "teddy bear."

In 1905 the first of the "literary" teddy bears made its debut. English writer Paul Piper (writing as Seymour Eaton) wrote a series of books about "The Roosevelt Bears" that stimulated a flow of commercial products, including stuffed bears called "Teddy G" (for gray) and "Teddy B" (for brown). These were the first in a continuing tradition of literary-cum-toy bears that includes Pooh, Paddington, Little Bear, Yogi, and Smokey.

Antique Bears

By Kim Brewer

The Antique
Bear Market

ONWARD AND UPWARD

Eighty years have passed since an alarmed customs inspector in Kansas City reported that he had cleared the import papers of 609 bears, 5 goats, 6 cats, and other animals and that he feared "this place won't be fit to live in!" Worse was yet to come—he was informed that 15,000 other bears had already been inspected. "It will be positively dangerous to spend the winter in Kansas City!" was his chilling conclusion.

But he needn't have worried. Any child would have known that the "bears" were of the teddy bear variety and that they were probably intended for the Christmas stockings, not the highways and byways of Kansas City.

The interesting phenomenon that this reveals, however, is one we tend to forget today. And that is that the teddy bear was big business in the first decade of the 20th century, in spite of annual predictions that the bottom would drop out "next year."

In 1907 it was reported by *Playthings* that teddy bear factories could be found in practically every big city in America, and it urged buyers to order early to be sure of having an adequate supply. "We stand firmly in the belief that bears have come to stay," they announced, "and that sales this year, at all seasons and at any particular season, will be better than last year."

Sales were high, but prices—by today's standards—were appealingly low. For example, you could buy a dozen 18-inch teddy bears "all having voices" for only $18 from Steinfield Bros. in New York in 1907. (A dozen 8-inch bears cost only $4.80.)

A mammoth 21-inch-high bear on wheels sold for only $7.50 in the same year; and bear offers abounded, luring children to sell orders of magazines or bluing or other products in return for a free teddy.

We know now that the teddy bear market has continued to grow as the century has progressed, and that little girls—and boys—and their parents are often enthusiastic collectors of bears with no apparent damage to their parental instincts.

The chances of finding a mint-condition antique bear for a bargain price at a flea market or auction, either here or in Europe, has become more and more remote; but the possibility of finding an exact replica of an antique bear is becoming more promising. This is because there are modern bear artists and bearmakers whose extraordinary artistry creates handcrafted bears of great beauty and distinctiveness. Some are replicas of antique bruins; others are entirely original. Many are signed and numbered, assuring their value as collectors' delights.

The antique bear market and the modern artist bear market are reflections of each other. One inspires the vision of the other; both fulfill the needs of collectors—and the longings of children. Together they form an expanding market with a wonderful history and a bright future.

MARKET TRENDS

Experts from several auction houses and a long-time dealer shared their latest predictions about where the market for teddy bears is heading.

❧

Emma Hill of the Phillips Auction Gallery in London believes that the teddy bear phenomenon "is absolutely amazing. The prices they are fetching are just incredible. People are probably buying them because of their tremendous nostalgic value, to hold onto a bit of what's gone before. We see this in the toy market in general, although there is something special about a teddy bear. Somehow it becomes almost human—something you don't find with other toys.

"With regard to the future of the market, I simply don't know. The whole nature of teddy bear collecting is so unscientific that I don't think anyone can make tremendous predictions about it. Some things fetch a lot of money and then, ten years later, nothing. Right now teddy bears are so high, one almost wonders if it can go on. It certainly hasn't tailed off yet. As there exists only a limited supply of antique teddy bears, they may just continue to go on full strength for some time!"

❧

Ms. Hill's associate at Phillips in New York, Henry Kurtz, has written the definitive book about toy soldiers, his specialty. He has researched the work of European toymakers for decades and notes how they maintain rigidly high standards of design, execution, and more detailed painting. He also points out that many American toymakers have been of German and European extraction.

In the last few years Phillips Auction Gallery has seen a definite increase in interest and strong following for teddy bears, Steiff in particular. In 1987, for example, a 16-inch Steiff "Jackie" realized an unexpected auction price of $1,500. Its presale estimate was $500 to $700. Mr. Kurtz sees English teddy bears appreciating in value and believes that eventually they will perform as well as Steiff in American auctions.

❧

Bunny Campione, a consultant to the Collectors' Department at Sotheby's in London, tells how she fell in love with her first bear: "I started auctioning teddy bears in 1982 with a large collection of mainly English bears. A black bear in the sale realized £350, which I believe was the highest price ever paid at auction. I fell in love with it! The next sale, in 1983, saw a Steiff bear realize £1,300, a new record. Subsequent sales— at least one a year—have set new world records. In 1987 a white-muzzled Steiff went for £8,800. This record was not beaten until recently, when the Steiff bear was sold for £55,000.

"I foresee that English bears, such as Chad Valley, Merrythought, Farnell, and Chiltern, will rise to the upper hundreds, providing they are in great condition with their tag or button trademarks intact. However, I do not feel they will reach the Steiff levels for a few more years.

"As more bears come on the market, their condition becomes more and more important to increasingly discerning collectors. Where a glass eye can be replaced without much change to the value of a bear, an ear cannot, nor can fur. Fur is a major factor."

❧

Christie's London started selling teddy bears "seriously" in 1983, according to Olivia Bristol. "I noticed that as people really got interested, prices took off. When offered a large teddy bear collection, we decided to hold our first ever teddy bear and soft toy sale. That was in December

1984. The media response was incredible. We had nine television stations represented in the room, with barely two yards of space for each. They were queued up outside on the pavement at half past eight in the morning, fighting for a place. It was very exciting. Nothing like that had happened before, and we were really amazed at the interest. At first we thought it a sort of phenomenon, that it wouldn't last; but people are still buying. There are very serious collectors. A good bear (an early Steiff bear in good condition and rare color) will bring £10,000 or £15,000.

"Although the future of the bear market is difficult to predict, we suspect the top-quality bears will hold their value. Even the cheaper end of the market—Chad Valley, Merrythought, and 1950s bears—are now bringing £100 or £150. And those can still be picked up at jumble sales for 10p. So it's quite an interesting market.

"Recently someone brought a red bear to the Russian department of our head office. When it arrived at South Kensington, I absolutely flipped, knowing it was wonderful before learning just how special it was.

"Our research showed it had belonged to a Russian royal princess. Her mother was a first cousin and good friend of King George V. In 1914 the princess came to spend a summer holiday at Buckingham Palace. Then, of course, war broke out, and she couldn't return. In 1919 she was staying somewhere in London when her father was assassinated by the Bolsheviks. We believe the bear was a gift from her father, and she kept it as a souvenir of him. I rang up the Steiff Company, but they didn't have any record of a line of red teddy bears. As we know, it is a Steiff, with the traditional look and a button in the ear. Steiff decided that it must have been a special order placed by her father and that perhaps as many as six were produced, but I've never seen another. This one is in very good condition. The original Russian peasant costume protected the mohair underneath.

"The bear was auctioned in May 1989 and brought £12,000, setting a new world record!"

❧

Grace Dyar, a full-time antique dealer, is considered the "Grand Dame of dolldom." She has written about and lectured on dolls for more than 60 years, is a consultant to several doll museums, and commands the respect of the doll world. She had some interesting thoughts about where the market is going.

Asked if she thought recent record prices for teddy bears meant that bears were becoming more popular than dolls for collectors, she wouldn't go quite that far; but she did feel that the record auction prices "have changed the way people feel about the market. They have to be exceedingly careful. Prices are so high, and people are always hopeful that what they have to sell or want to buy is one of the record breakers."

Today, people are spending as much or more for reproductions of antique bears as they are for the genuine antique. The only time this is a problem is when both the dealer and buyer assume that the bear is an antique and they do not have enough information to properly identify its origins. (It should be noted that modern bear artists doing originals or reproductions sign and label their work.) In the chapters that follow you will find more information on how to make an informed purchase.

Have prices slacked off somewhat in recent months? "I believe they have for bears that are not of the highest quality," Dyar said. "I was trying to sell a 'played-with' bear for some people. It was not blue-ribbon quality but was a nice collector's item. I wasn't able to sell it for as high a price as the owners thought it would bring. Some years ago," she continued, "that bear would have seemed more appealing. Then people more or less 'bought with their memories' and their hearts, rather than thinking about their pocketbooks. It's all relative, of course. Everything is escalating."

When asked what she thought about the billion-dollar industry for new toy bears in the United States, she was quick to praise it: "I think some of the new bears are really terrific! Most of them are so well done that they are sure to be future collectors' items—depending on how many are made, of course." What should a purchaser look for in a new bear? "The way they join the seams is very important," she noted: "Look for the ones that are as sturdy and well made as our old bears were. And look for the ones that have that 'knowledgeable look' that makes so many antique bears appealing. That's very important. Some bears look as if they could speak!"

Materials are not the prime consideration in choosing a new bear, Dyar believes. "But I think natural materials look better and are probably more durable and a better investment than synthetics."

When asked how she would advise a collector who is about to spend several hundred dollars for a bear that might turn out to be a reproduction, Dyar said:

"Well, I think a sincere dealer should give purchasers the privilege of thinking over the purchase for at least a day and of having the option of returning it if they change their minds. This return policy should also apply to sales to dealers. We can't put a value on sentiment. Sometimes a person sells a piece to a dealer and then finds out it had special value for another member of his family, or something like that, and wants to buy it back. I think a reputable dealer should be willing to give a written guarantee that the seller can buy the bear back within a limited period of time—a day or two—if he wants to."

Her final word to the collector of antique bears is to study both antique and modern bears and become as well informed as possible on the subject. "A true antique bear will always be worth as much as or more than you paid for it," she noted, "especially if you didn't overpay for it and if you take reasonable care to preserve it. Don't store it where it can be made love to by moths!" she advised. Then she added: "Actually, carpet beetles are most likely to damage a teddy bear, you know."

What Determines Price?

There are several criteria that knowledgeable collectors and dealers can apply when deciding how much to pay for a teddy bear. Among these are *condition, rarity, color, regional preferences, provenance, and personality*. Let's look at each in turn:

Condition. It is obvious that a bear in excellent condition—all original parts, little wear, etc.—will be priced at the top end of each category, whereas the bear with a "sorrow"—in a much-loved and worn condition—will be at the lower end.

Of critical concern to the serious teddy collector today is the condition, type, and length of the mohair "fur." A bear with a luxurious pelt will nearly always command a higher price than his balding brother. Even with two fully furred and otherwise equal bears, the one with the longer mohair will rise to the top of the price range.

In 1985 the Amherst Teddy Bear Rally was the site of two important transactions. In one, a 19-inch Steiff bear sold for $1,900, and a smaller, 14-inch bear of the same color and virtually the same condition brought an amazing $3,000. The difference? The smaller bear's mohair was almost twice as long as his big brother's.

In 1982 I bought a 17-inch Steiff bear at Withington's auction for a fairly reasonable $700. The next year I sent an identical bear in equal overall condition—but with shorter mohair—to a well-advertised West Coast auction, where it did not sell for quite half that price.

Rarity. Although mint condition is usually a prediction of premium price, an important corollary is rarity, or the frequency with which a certain bear appears on the market. If 20,000 bears of a certain type were manufactured but only a handful ever appear for sale, they are considered rare, and their price will rise accordingly. The bottom can drop out quickly, though, when a pack of identical bruins comes to market. This happened in 1983 when a huge Steiff display bear brought $9,000. Suddenly, four more surfaced and were sold. When a sixth—in mint condition—was put up for sale at a prestigious auction house, it went for only a fraction of the price of the first one. Why? It was no longer a "rarity."

However, rarity can be preserved even when a veritable treasure trove is unearthed. In 1982 an entire warehouse lot of "mint-in-box" mechanical Peter Bears (manufactured in 1925) was found by a Connecticut dealer. Sold to only a few selected dealers, the bears were conservatively dispersed to the market over a period of years, thus ensuring their rarity and value.

Color. A horse of a different color is a rarity, and bears of a different color—lavender, black, or red, for example—are among the most sought-after toys in the world, leaving their cinnamon, beige, and golden brother bears in the dust.

When a lavender Chad Valley bear went up for auction at Marvin Cohen's in 1986, tremendous excitement built as the bidding rose to $600. A little earlier in the same auction, a bear that was identical, except that it was golden in color, had brought only $110!

At Christie's in New York in 1987, a beautiful 14-inch white Steiff bear sold for a stunning $4,000 before buyer's premium. This same bear was immediately resold to another dealer and then quickly sold to a third, and each time the price rose higher. Meanwhile, back at the ranch in Brimfield, Massachusetts, more than 25 Steiff bears with similar credentials remained unsold at a price range of $700 to $1,000. Why? They were a common beige color.

Schuco miniature bears are great ambassadors of color, traveling from collector to collector in their elegant deep cinnamon and bright orange furs, rarely pausing to be admired on a dealer's shelf. Mechanical Schuco bears, especially in turquoise and kelly green, are a toy dealer's dream. Recently a lavender "Tumbler" sold for $2,000, despite its diminutive size, and a lavender "Perfume" in its original shade and condition was plucked by a British fancier for $2,200. Color, in these cases, was obviously the reason for the high prices because at the same time a Midwestern dealer tried unsuccessfully to sell a "Compact" Schuco mechanical bear at the Atlantic City Show for $500 and finally sold it for a slightly lower price a year later. The bear was a common color.

Mechanical Peter bears in rare colors have been sold by telephone, sight unseen, on several occasions. They are so desirable that they rarely appear on the open market, and to advertise one in a publication is usually to sell it within 24 hours.

Colorful bears, as you can see, have it "made in the shade"!

Regional preferences. There are regional preferences and even U.S. versus European preferences for different kinds of bears, and these are reflected by wide variations in price from place to place. For example, New Englanders cherish miniature bears. Mechanical bruins command markedly higher prices throughout Massachusetts, New York, and the northernmost states. In California the big market is for medium-size bears and Hollywood-size display pieces. It is risky to generalize about who loves antique bears the most, but it is a fact that most of the top prices for antique bears before 1985 were paid on the East Coast.

Since 1985, prices in Europe have skyrocketed: a Schuco "Perfume" priced in the United States at $500 would bring $1,000 in England. Dealers and collectors are learning, with difficulty, to live with this international disparity. And they must also adjust to the fact that the Northeast corridor of the United States is a true "bear market," where the game seems to call for records to be topped at each sale.

Provenance. Because teddy bears are usually family pets before they become collectors' items, most would have long and interesting stories to tell if they could just talk! It is natural, therefore, to put a higher value on a bear whose owner was a famous person or who participated in some historical event. Imagine owning Christopher Milne's Pooh! (The original Pooh Bear, by the way, is greeting friends at his new home in the children's room of the Donnell branch of the New York Public Library.) In May 1989 a much-worn little bear that a cousin of Czar Nicholas II once played with brought the highest price then paid for a bear: nearly $20,000. As with all antiques, a provenance that documents where it has been and who has owned it is a valuable asset for a teddy.

Personality. That certain something that makes you want to hug him— a crooked mouth, ears that beg to be fondled—every bear has a personality that is uniquely his own. It is hard to put a monetary value on so abstract a feature, but every "bearophile" understands the special appeal that attracts and captivates the buyer and lures him on to higher and higher limits. Be aware, though, that buying an "investment" bear for its personality alone can be risky if it lacks other more measurable qualities. However, if the bear really exerted his charms for you alone, who can say whether you made a mistake by taking him home with you, whatever the cost?

Price per inch. For years I supplied bear dealers and pickers with a sliding scale showing how various factors affected what I would pay for antique teddies. The graphs had columns for percentage of mohair, color of mohair, and height of bear. Later I incorporated columns for length of arm and size of foot. It was an interesting concept but doomed to failure because of wide variations in human perceptions!

In one instance I bought a white bear for top dollar sight unseen because the auctioneer who described it to me as of pristine quality could not see the slight patches of mohair missing all over the toy and the stained shade of "white."

Years of controversial encounters over the queries about colors, hair content, and age of bears have helped me develop a foolproof method for buying by phone or mail. I now request a perusal/return grace period and will buy a bear only from excellent photos or close personal examination. Return privileges are essential, even from auction houses, and whenever possible I try to find out the identity of my underbidder if I am not present at the auction itself. This knowledge is useful and often enlightening. Some auctioneers are happy to supply this information, but they are not required to do so.

Once you have your hands on the bear, the primary concerns for price differentials are general condition, amount of mohair present, length of mohair, regional preferences, color, and size.

Bears are measured from the top of the head to the heel. Do not measure from the ears because ears can stand several inches above the skull peak.

A toy is considered "mint-in-box" when it retains all of its original tags, pamphlets, and so on, and is virtually unplayed with.

Fakes

The current popularity of teddy bears has made the reproduction—and faking—of antique bears into a lucrative business. Along with the public's willingness to pay high prices for good reproductions came an awareness of the tremendous potential for forgeries passed off as original. As is the case with other collectibles, such as Tiffany lamps and folk art, forgeries

A German teddy on board a 1905 American steed carved by German-born craftsman Daniel C. Muller. *From the collection of Lynn Trusdell.*

13

have become so prevalent in the last few years that there is a need for some basic guidelines to help the purchaser separate the real from the fake antique.

When purchasing an old bear, in particular one that has no noticeable restoration, look at the pads for tell-tale hints of fraud. Most fakes lack overall wear on the pads but instead exhibit dark-stained central sections only. Many fakers use leather to eliminate this problem, but you should know that leather was rarely used on old bears. One fraudulent Ideal bear purchased in 1985 for $750 had been "christened" in herb and clove scents that gave it a suspiciously unauthentic aroma. Old bears have a unique odor that comes from the combination of old straw, wood shavings, and the canvas and mohair fabric.

Lately, I have seen several examples of "wear" made by crude horizontal scissor cuts on some carefully formed bears. Uneven wear and

Fake Ideal teddy, Fairfield, Maine.

thick-ended mohair tufts revealed the fact of mechanical distress rather than of natural wear.

Noses in the fake teddies are often too thick in thread, and the thread is sometimes dark in color instead of worn to a grayish color. Eyes are often tiny old shoe buttons because authentic glass eyes and large old shoe buttons are difficult to obtain. One giveaway is the turn of the seam on the newly produced critter. In many cases fur on old bears, Steiff in particular, is carefully plucked out of the seams, and a fluffy, even appearance is evident on the seam line. Repros' seams are usually clumped with mohair, the result of hasty handiwork.

Stuffing is not often a good indicator of falsified goods. Some fine old bears are restuffed with nylon stockings, cotton, and acrylic. Over the years some collectors have indicated to me that a certain percentage of restuffing is acceptable; the advanced collector may prefer to buy bears without any stuffing if the discs, seams, and other elements are original.

In 1988 a western Massachusetts dealer purchased a fake American-style bear for a great sum, only to find that the discs and pins were plastic. After these factors were discovered, it became obvious that the entire bear was fake. These parts are almost impossible to reproduce.

In the case of fraud, the dealer is responsible for compensation and/or proof that the item is indeed exactly as represented. In parts of Europe, fraud is a crime punishable by imprisonment and large fines. Consequently, the incidence of fraud in teddy bear sales has decreased substantially there. To date, the United States has no analogous restrictions.

Restoring a Bear

PROFESSIONAL BEAR RESTORERS

Regina Brock is a teddy bear artist; Sue Foskey creates reproduction bears from antique mohair; and Louise Laskey is an artist, sculptor, and collector of bears and other toys.

In addition, all three have become widely known as restorers of antique bears, and their stories are full of the techniques and philosophy of bear repair.

❧

Regina Brock considers the creation of her art bears to be her primary career, but over the past few years she has accepted the challenge of restoring several particularly valuable old bruins to their original beauty.

One technique she has developed is the replacement of mohair, strand by strand, into a worn bear's cloth. The process is reversible, should anyone want to strip the bear to its original materials later on. Regina's arduous task of refurring a bear begins by counting the number of hairs per tuft in the original mohair and then inserting new hairs to match both the "lay" of the original as well as the color. Although this is an extremely time-consuming and therefore expensive process, Regina feels that because old bears in good condition are becoming scarcer, more people are willing to spend large amounts of money to preserve important bears.

She notes, however, that a bear with added fur must be labeled as such when it is sold, and dealers should make full disclosure to the buyer of any other alterations that have been made. "How to calculate value on a

16

percentage basis when the entire bear is no longer original can pose an ethical dilemma for the dealer," she says.

She points out that many antiques are good candidates for restoration, especially when such repairs ensure the preservation of the item or restore its function. Imagine, for example, a Queen Anne tea table with a cracked leg or a vintage car whose engine needs some replacement parts to put it in running order. In the same way, a bear damaged by water or insect attacks or threatened by falling limbs can be saved and often much improved by loving and careful restoration.

Collectors are accustomed to the normal effects of loving and hugging on old bears; they are charmed by the unique postures and personalities that result from such careless caring and would not wish to erase these well-earned marks.

Regina's advice about restoration is to go ahead with restoration if the bear's appearance and salability are important because restoration, reversibly executed, will improve both.

❧❧

Sue Foskey has seen a lot of bears whose value has been lost through careless repairing. Glue, plastic eyes, and applied noses are among the horrors she has found, and she is quick to caution against such quick-fix repairs.

"The value of a bear will always increase if repairs are properly done," she says. "The first thing I check for when starting to restore a bear is the extent of dry rot in the fabric. This occurs most often in bears that have been stuffed with wood wool from softwood trees whose acidity encourages the fabric to rot. If I find that the rot is too extensive or the fabric too fragile, I will suggest to the owner that the bear be dressed to hide its wounds rather than try to repair it."

Sue will not replace antique "growlers," the voice of a teddy, except at the owner's insistence. She will mend and repack them as well as she can, however.

Repairs range from recovering pads (the most common repair) to rejoining separated limbs. If replacement of a part is needed, Sue uses only antique materials.

❧❧

Louise Laskey started restoring teddy bears and old Steiff animals for dealers more than a decade ago. At her Teddy Bear Hospital she tries to prolong the life of antique teddies without destroying their "nice old looks." She had done much research into the history of materials and manufacturing companies, so her restoration is as authentic as possible.

These materials sometimes come from unlikely places. Taxidermists were once Louise's only source of glass eyes and long needles for toy repairs; kapok (silky fibers from the ceiba tree), used as stuffing by some English bearmakers and as padding around a growler or squeaker, used to be available from upholsterers. Later she found a source in old life preservers whose sections were stuffed with kapok.

Mohair, a fabric made of the long silky hairs of the angora goat, can be purchased in various lengths, textures, and colors; but the bear restorer must use a lot of ingenuity in dyeing and "distressing" new material to match old.

Replacing pads is the most common repair needed by old bears. Although she is "filled with admiration" for the creative mothers who stitched on pieces of lisle stockings or made crocheted replacement pads for their children's bears, she herself will stick as closely as possible to the original material, shape, and color. Felt is the usual material, although some English bears had pads made of velvet, tarpaulin, or oilcloth. Some bears had claws embroidered on their paws, and these are restored also.

Should a bear be cleaned? Louise thinks a gentle vacuuming and brushing can do more good than harm by removing abrasive dirt and insect-attracting soil. She will also gently shampoo and fluff-dry bears with her special formula.

Can all bears be saved? Obviously, there are terminal cases among bears that have had one adventure too many. But parts of old bears can be salvaged to help restore others, and some really sad bears can be dressed to protect their fragility and prolong their lives for a while longer.

"I meet a lot of wonderful old bears in my business," says Louise, "and they bring along a lot of marvelous people."

A REVERSIBLE METHOD OF "RESTORING" MOHAIR ON ANTIQUE TEDDIES

In 1987 I was offered a large reddish Steiff teddy bear with one of the most endearing faces I'd seen. Initially this bear, which I call the "Rossetti Bear," seemed perfect, but closer inspection revealed a spotty loss of hair on front and back legs and a loss of roughly 90 percent of the back mohair.

Sparse mohair on his back seriously lessened his value, and because he was then offered for the "stilted" price of $1,200, I hesitated to purchase him.

For a year the bear sat in the back of a cedar closet. Then I was invited to appraise at a bear convention, and one of its promoters told me of an artist named Regina Brock, who was creating bears by weaving and piling raw mohair tufts into canvas bodies. When she demonstrated this procedure, I realized it could be used to weave mohair onto antique bears as well.

I commissioned Mrs. Brock to match-dye and repile the Rossetti bear as a last resort because the loss of mohair prevented his sale, even though his coloring was rare and unusual. This was probably why the fur had disappeared; the dye for pre-1920 "red" Steiffs contains a particularly tasty ingredient insects seem to like.

Regina returned him a year later, and his condition was extraordinary. There was no evidence of patchiness or indication of where the newly added patches were. And to my knowledge, this is the first time an antique bear had been restored in this manner. Since very few claret-colored Steiffs have passed through dealers' hands over the years, this particular bear was worth the time and effort and expense of repiling. His original value has more than doubled because of an excellent restoration.

ON RESTORING FUR IN AN ANTIQUE BEAR

Regina Brock's process of retufting the mohair into an old bear is a variation on the basic technique she developed in making her own bears. It is

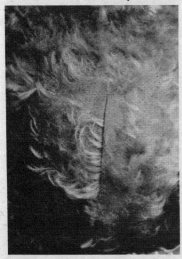

Rosetti, a 1903 Steiff red bear before the Brock treatment

. . . and after repiling of fur.

modified, however, to create the same appearance as the bear's original fur, and a museum-quality restoration is essential to me.

It is important to achieve a perfect color match, which usually involves a blending of two, three, or more colors. An old bear can require various tones and shades, depending on the areas where he may be faded or still retaining his original saturation of color.

The insertion of the mohair into the cloth must be in the same direction as the original piling on the bear. Any variation will be quickly detected and must be removed and retufted if necessary. Texture also must be matched.

Another extremely important aspect is matching the exact count of strands per tuft as in the bear's original fur. However, it is always safer to work with fewer strands in the needle instead of more.

TUFTING OF THE
LINEN/MOHAIR BEAR SEQUENCE

The following photographs illustrate Regina Brock's technique of tufting the mohair into the linen base surface of the conventionally constructed

A Brock bear prior to tufting.   Finally, the head is complete with 100% mohair threads.

Three stages in Regina Brock's tufting process. A new bear is shown for clarity. The process is the same for antique bruins. *Photos courtesy of Regina Brock.*

and jointed linen/mohair bear. This process seems to transform metamorphically as hundreds of passes and insertions of the needle gradually develop its long and dense coat of fur.

Each tuft of mohair is threaded through a large-eye needle and sewn into the fabric surface, using hidden stitching methods to minimize the visibility of the rooting process. All tufting must be securely rooted into the cloth.

When done correctly, the retufting can strengthen the fabric as it becomes part of the weave itself but still invisible. It is important to mention that, if desired, any retufted areas can be removed without harming the fabric of the bear.

It is not a process that can be hurried, and this type of handwork requires love and patience. It is tremendously rewarding to bring a bear back to its almost original condition and to know its life has been lengthened. Not all bears will be candidates for this type of treatment, and respecting the "personal history" of a bear, recorded in the condition of his appearance, must always be considered for those collectors who prefer their bear found that special way; for every bear has a story and deserves the right to let it be known he was very much loved.

Repairing a Bear

Now that you've read what three professionals say about bear repairs, you may want to try your own skills.

A word of caution before you begin, however: *All restoration should be totally reversible, especially if the bear has any value as an antique.* And as a corollary: *A part should not be replaced unless there is no possible way to salvage it.*

PADS

Pads are an exception to this rule. If the damage is so extensive that it cannot be salvaged, it would warrant complete removal and replacement. Hopefully, only one pad has to be removed. However, keep in mind that replacing will ultimately lower the value of the bear. The decision to replace a pad is a very personal one. When removing the antique pads, be very careful that the edge of the hem mohair is not ripped. Even minor ripping can cause the loss of an inch or so in height, and with current price-per-inch valuations for antique teddies, it would be preferable to have a taller bear with old, damaged pads than a shorter bear with new feet!

Here's how the professionals do it:

Step 1: Remove all of the pad and trim edging as closely to the original as possible, but leave the original thick-sewn margin. This allows the pad to take the strong pulling by the thread required to achieve its original appearance. Save any cardboard platform you may find inside.

Step 2: Place tracing paper across the newly opened foot and trace the edge of the foot with a marker until the correct pad size is clearly drawn. Be very careful not to make any marks on the bear.

Step 3: Place pre-tinted pad fabric—canvas or wool felt—flat on table. Pin tracing paper on pad fabric and cut around the marked area, leaving a 1/4-inch margin all around for the new hem. Make sure foot proportions are not distorted by a shift in the stuffing and that the width of the foot remains as narrow as the ankle measurement.

Step 4: Reverse pad fabric and place on top of the foot. Starting at the toe, carefully pin the pad fabric to the foot along the margins, working halfway to the heel on each side. Do not go past the midway mark or you will not be able to turn the sewn section inside out.

Step 5: Sew, with cotton thread, using tiny regular stitches, beginning at the toe. Check the width against the old stuffing as you go. It may be necessary to adjust the old stuffing to fill the toe firmly. Original stuffing is sometimes difficult to manipulate into the new pad.

Step 6: Turn the pad and fold under the remaining hem. Pin it all the way to the heel, maintaining its original width to the curve of the heel.

Step 7: Sew from the midsection, using the parallel stitch illustrated. This stitch is undetectable and will finish the pad.

Step 8: When all sewing and shaping are completed, take a hard toothbrush and rub around the rim of the pad to pull out old mohair that you may have sewn under.

Step 9: The new pad can be tinted to match the old ones by using commercial dyes or tea. Use a color-coding chart or a piece of the old pad as a guide for this work. This should be done before sewing the pads on the bear.

Note: If you find a cardboard form when you remove the old pad, it should be reused and placed over the stuffing and under the new pad. It also may be useful in determining the size and shape of the new pad. Cardboards were often used for foot platforms in large Steiff bears and in some American bears as well.

EARS

Ear repair is the simplest of bear operations because many ears need simply a few stitches to tack them into place. To determine the original placement of dislocated ears, try first to find remnants of old thread lodged near the bear's temples.

The position of a bear's ears is a clue to his origins: Don't give an American bear a German accent by setting his ears at the wrong angle— or vice versa! If you're in doubt about his original appearance, try to find pictures or an expert to help you.

The Steiff ear, in most cases, is sewn into the temple seam when the bear is being formed and is therefore difficult to replace. Its distinctive positioning is a trademark of the company and should be maintained. The ears are set off the outside of the temple seam, then curve to the right on the right side and to the left on the left side, toward the front. In situations where a valuable Steiff is in need of an ear, and old mohair is difficult to obtain, some resourceful renovators have excised small pieces from the back of the bear to provide a section of the ear. However, all other possibilities should be exhausted before resorting to this kind of surgery, and new mohair is generally preferred.

A word about replacement of the Steiff "button in the ear." There is evidence that fraudulent Steiff buttons have been placed in all manner of toys, even American, English, and other European bears. A replaced button is not a guarantee of date or authenticity unless other positive identification can be made.

RESTUFFING

If you decide to restuff your sagging bruin, you may be surprised at what you find inside! Although fine wood shavings is the filling preferred by most manufacturers, some amazing products can emerge from the bodies of even classic teddies. Bearmakers sometimes resorted to handy leftovers— unlikely substances such as old shirts, cotton stripping, felt wadding, and even horse or poodle hair. Also, it is not uncommon for a bear to have undergone a midlife restuffing with whatever materials the bear's well-meaning restorer could quickly lay hands on.

When restuffing your antique teddy, it is advisable to consider the fragility of the old fabric before you begin. One way to check this is to poke lightly into several parts of the bear with your finger. If the fabric is still strong enough to cover a football, the bear is ready for a filling meal of wood wool. However, if some weakness is observed or the weave is separating, a lighter, softer stuffing can be substituted. One type of material is nylon stockings, which can be easily poked into small openings anywhere on the bear. The purist might argue about inserting modern materials in an antique body, but, in fact, few collectors object when told that their new purchase has been restuffed with a "soft fiber." Nylon stuffing has the additional advantage of drying very quickly, which helps offset the dry rot that mohair is susceptible to when it must endure damp conditions. However, it should be noted that bears have been known to split open if overstuffed with modern materials.

BATHS AND DECONTAMINATION

When you buy an old bear, you might want to put him in an "isolation ward" for several days to be sure he hasn't brought pests along with him that could spread to other bears in your collection. An antique teddy's body, with its mohair and wood and years of accumulated "loving," is an excellent host for all kinds of unwelcome parasites.

My favorite treatment consists of spraying the inside surfaces of an airtight box or garbage bag with a commercial insect repellent and then sealing the bear inside for three or four days. (Be careful that the bear does not touch the sprayed surface.) When he emerges from solitary confinement, the bear is ready for his bath.

Bathing should be done as soon as possible after debugging the bear in order to remove all traces of residual oils and toxins. If the bear is exposed to sunlight while these chemicals are still present, the mohair will become sensitized and fade more quickly.

Always use extreme caution when bathing a bear. Be sure to avoid getting water on the bear's pads during his bath. Original pads are often made of highly absorbent wool felt that will become water-stained or that will pill or even tear when wet.

Teddies made from materials such as cotton plush or acrylic or other synthetic fibers should not be bathed without consulting a reputable dry cleaner first. Irreversible matting could result from such a bath. Plush is defined as a fabric with an even pile, longer and less dense than velvet. Mohair, which is used on most antique bears, usually has an uneven, curly pile (except when it has been shaved), and it is safe to bathe a mohair bear by using the careful method described below:

To prepare for the cleaning, you will need

1. A measuring cup of warm water.
2. Suds of the mildest soap (good products are often found at teddy bear conventions).
3. A washcloth—*not* a sponge.

4. A hair dryer with stationary mount (to be used on cool temperature only).

Blow or brush off excess dust and dirt. Then lightly moisten the ends of the hairs (not the canvas backing) in a 1- to 3-inch area with the washcloth dampened in *clean* hot water. Now dip the cloth in *soapy* hot water, wring it out, and go over the moistened area again, using circular motions. Rinse with the cloth wrung out in the clear water.

Caution: If at any time you begin to see a markedly darker tone emerge, stop. This is a sign that the stuffing is bleeding into the mohair backing. At this point take a piece of dry terry cloth and rub the damp spot in a circular motion to dry it quickly. Bleeding can be a particularly disturbing problem on white or cream-colored bears, and a test spot on some hidden part of the torso is advisable before bathing the entire bear.

Once a light-colored bear is stained from the dyes used in the stuffing or cardboard forms, there is no way to restore the pristine color. Mohair cannot be bleached without irreparable damage.

When cleaning is complete, fluff and dry your freshly scrubbed teddy in front of a gentle breeze from the hair dryer.

MECHANICAL REPAIRS

Squeakers are essentially small, circular or lozenge-shaped bellows inside the stomach or under the arms of a bear; they give the bear his voice when squeezed. Very few antique bears have squeakers that still function, but they can be repaired. Old Steiff squeakers were often made of gessoed canvas and animal glue. The canvas was glued to two wooden disks with a spring between them, and a small hole allowed the air to escape with a woodwind sound when the bellows was squeezed. With use and over time, the glue holding the canvas to the disks gives out, and the bellows loses its power. Repair usually involves relocating the spring and regluing the canvas.

Growler or *rocker* mechanisms are activated by pulling on a string or by rocking the bear forward and backward. In a standing bear, the back can be opened, and a new piece of string can be attached. Be sure, however, that the new string is the same thickness as the original one or it will not slip in and out of its hole easily. (I learned this the hard way when, after two weeks of work on restoring a 36-inch bear on wheels, I discovered that the new string was too thick, and I had to redo the whole process!)

REALIGNING THE BEAR ON WHEELS

This can be a risky business for the inexperienced. The antique armature inside such bears is often welded, and if it is bent or broken, it must be repaired by welding. Needless to say, risks of fire damage or total destruction of the bear are present whenever the heat or sparks of the welding tool come close to the aged fabric and stuffing. This is a repair best left to the professional, who will have to remove the stuffing nearest the area to be repaired and protect the rest with fireproof material. It is an expensive and time-consuming process and may not be worth the visual difference in the end. Some weaknesses in the mechanism can, of course, be corrected from the outside, and these should always be attempted first.

How to Use This Section

This guide is a manual for the beginning as well as the advanced collector. It will also be useful to the dealer in general antiques who wants a quick price reference for buying privately or at auctions or flea markets.

In using this guide, please keep in mind that teddy bears, unlike dolls, are not cast from molds! Teddy bears are often unmarked and may show little resemblance to others of the same company origin or with similar tags. A teddy bear has a distinct personality, which not only affects his appeal but his ultimate price as well.

In this book we have made every effort to provide accurate retail price ranges. These ranges are based on realized prices over the past five years.

The problem with price ranges is that no sector of the market buys exclusively retail or wholesale. Therefore, these prices reflect a mix of collectors and dealers at both the buying end and the selling end of the spectrum. It is considered an acceptable practice for a dealer to purchase an item for a fraction ($1/3$ to $2/3$) of its retail value. But a dealer in fine toys may purchase unusually good pieces at a retail price because he has a loyal group of customers who trust that his cumulative experience and instincts can be relied on. Whatever price he feels is fair may seem high to the casual observer, yet, in fact, it is fair when judged by those who really know this specialized market.

When a dealer pays a record price at auction, for example, it may be because his working knowledge of the market and his feel for the rarity of the item give him a special insight on values. On the other hand, a lucky private collector may come across a rare or mint-quality bear hiding in an attic or in grandmother's trunk and be able to purchase it for close to the wholesale price without paying a dealer's premium.

American Bears

Until quite recently it has been virtually impossible to identify antique bears of American origin. One of the reasons is that American bears in the early years of the century were almost never marked by their manufacturers. Sometimes it is this absence of any tags that most clearly points to an American bear. But to determine the company that made it is an additional problem.

In some cases definite attributions have been made through the fortunate combination of historic documentation and company records, as in the identification of the Teddy Roosevelt campaign teddies as Ideal Toy Company bears.

The American bears pictured in this section are the best examples we could find, and the prices represent this high caliber of condition and rarity.

GUND

An American company founded by a German, Gund Manufacturing Co. began in Norwalk, Connecticut, in 1898. In 1910 Adolf Gund went into partnership with Jacob Swedlin and moved the company to New York City. When Gund retired in 1922, Swedlin continued to head it. Gund has made bears since at least 1927, when it advertised a line of "silk plush bears." It also made bears on wheels large enough for a child to ride on.

IDEAL TOY COMPANY

The Ideal Toy Company makes claim, along with others, to have been the first company to make the teddy bear. However, the phenomenal success of the company has been due more to its original ideas and creative marketing than to any one product. It has acquired the licenses for innumerable toys from the movie and entertainment industry and has become a giant manufacturer with a modern plant in Newark, New Jersey, and subsidiary operations worldwide. The company went public in 1968 and was purchased by CBS, Inc., in 1982.

MISCELLANEOUS BEAR COMPANIES

A great many companies joined the teddy bear parade in the years following its emergence as a toy of enduring popularity. Such names as Oskar Buchner, E. Dehler, Josef Deuerlein, Fleischmann & Bloedel, Albert Forster, Hahn & Co., Carl Harmus, Leven & Sprenger, Andreas Muller, G. Schmey Nachf., Edvard Schmidt, Herman Steiner, and others testify to the quantities of German-made teddy bears produced.

In America countless companies began in response to the popularity of stuffed bears: The American Doll & Toy Manufacturers, Bruin Manufacturing Co., Hecla Bears, Harman Manufacturing Co., and Aetna Bears all provided competition for the imported German bears. With typical entrepreneurial spirit, the Americans also developed satellite products: accessories for bears—clothes and vehicles, for example; books about bears; ingenious musical and mechanical bears; and so on in a remarkable crescendo that continues to the present day.

AMERICAN BEAR PRICES

American, Ideal, 12", golden mohair. Firsthand accounts of two girls, now in their 80s, place this bear with the ambitious Roosevelt campaign around 1904. This is the model and painted "Googley eyed" Ideal that was thrown from trains into the waiting arms of elated children. Note the spear-shaped tops of the toes, a certain mark of the Ideal Company. It is likely that the few surviving examples of this bear lost the white and black top paint laid over the shoe button eyes. As yet, we have no absolute indication of the reason for the comical gesture.

   Value (with original painted eyes): $1,500-$2,000.

A premium investment example in folk art, political, historical, and Americana.

Antique Bear Pricing

Prices reflect actual sales by dealers and auction houses for the past five years.

American, Ideal style, 8". Charcoal to light gray tipped mohair (head, hands, feet), red, white, blue striped cotton body with two pom-poms. Shoe button eyes with red felt backs, black sewn nose, horizontal stitches, rust-colored claws. All jointed. Squeaker not functional. Black felt pads (worn).. Purchased from "picker" in 1983 for $35; resold same month for $600.
Value: $3,000 and up.

An important American bear example.

American, Ideal, "Perky" style, 13", 1907, beige mohair. Shoe button eyes, black sewn nose (horizontal stitching), mouth and claws (3). Very good overall condition with longer mohair, unusual to American specimens.

Value: $1,000-$1,500.

American, Ideal, 10", 1915, pale gold mohair. Button eyes. Medium-long silky mohair. Some extensive wear and pad loss.
Value: In good condition, $800-$1,200.

American, Ideal, 13", 1904, gold. Replaced pads. Wear throughout. Mohair. A good deal of facial hair is missing, but the marvelous "classic" Ideal
expression surpasses all limits here, and this bear was able to capture his
buyer in 1988 for a still reasonable $900.

Value: $1,000–$1,500.

American, unknown, 13", 1905. Triangular head, pointed toes on original pads. Short shaven mohair found in so many American bears. Shoe button eyes. Retains roughly 80% of his original fur. Exceptional face and good overall presence.

Value: $1,000-$1,500.

American, unknown, 11″, 1915, beige gold mohair. Shoe button eyes.
Squeaker not functional.
Value: $500-$1,000.

American, Ideal type, 10", 1910, beige mohair. Some stains on pads. Heavy wear on back. Purchased in 1986 for $350.
Value: $500-$1,000.

American, unknown, 14", 1910, blonde mohair. Clear glass eyes with black center. Pointed toes, full hump on back (which has no tuck). Cardboard filler under feet pads. Medium-length mohair in 90% condition.
Value: $1,000-$1,500.

American bear family, 1930, 4.25", 6.5", 7.5". Long black mohair with bright yellow gold glass eyes.
Value: $1,500–$2,500.

Antique Bear Pricing

Prices reflect actual sales by dealers and auction houses for the past five years.

American, 13", 1920, golden mohair. Shoe button eyes. Some slight wear. A beautiful example of the classic look in the 1920s. Some of these bears are sold in New York City and folk art galleries for over $800 (1988). Disproportionate eye size and tiny feet began to phase in on into the 1930s, with many New York "cottage industry" companies using blown-glass stickpins for eyes and scaling down the cost of the total bear by shortening arms and pad sizes.

Value: $300-$500.

Note: Bear collectors will rarely rise to the price folk art collectors will sometimes pay for this style of American teddy.

American, 15", 1920. This bear strongly resembles the preceding example. It is now believed that many of the lofts in New York City copied like
models and were fairly liberal with quality control. Some of these bears
were first seen in novelty shops along the northeast seaboard. They sold
for $6 per half dozen (smaller sizes).

Value: $350-$750.

American, Ideal, 12", 1905 on?, gold mohair. Good overall condition, displaying the extremely close shorn mohair and wide fabric piling seen in American used mohair. This bear has a red felt tongue. Tapering paws and feet that peak at the tip.

Value: $500-$1,000.

American, 10", 1905. This cute pure-white bear resembles some German bears of like time period. However, there is documentation that he is American, and his large torso and back hump are identical to American pre-1920s bears.

Value: $1,000-$1,500.

American, Character Toy Co., 18", 1941. Cinnamon mohair with large center seam in the face. Eyes have been replaced. This bear was very well loved and is still a precious possession to the lucky original owner. His velveteen pads and belly bear witness to a loyal companion. C. 1940s.

Value: With original owner's name and information, $125.

American, possibly Ideal, 20", 1917 on. In pristine condition. He was purchased in 1983 for $900 at the extravaganza in Pennsylvania. His new owner didn't bat an eyelid when she examined the exceptional condition and hard-to-find form.

Value: $1,500-$2,000.

American bear, Aetna, 25", 1907-20. Beautiful white mohair, remarkably well preserved; pads, glass eyes, nose all in excellent untouched condition.
Value: $1,700-$2,500.

Note: Large American bears are becoming equitable investments, with collectors recognizing rarity and the unique features of the U.S. teddy. A large white American bear with positive identification and origins will outshine many other collectible bears in many instances, and future investment potential is quite positive for any teddy ranking so highly in the categories of color, origin, and size.

Left. American, 1907-15; right, possibly German, 1907 on. Both bears are quite hairless (on the verge of complete baldness). All pads replaced. Repairs and stains throughout both torsos. Clothing can "make the bear" in some cases.
Value: Left, $200-$225 with clothes. Right, $125-$200.

American, Ideal, 22", 1904 on, gold. Short mohair. Near unplayed-with condition. Purchased in 1984 for $400, this bear was resold in 1985 for $2,800 in Baltimore.

Value: $2,500-$3,000.

American, 28", 1905-10. Bright gold with shoe button eyes. Mohair, all pads replaced.

Value: $600-$1,000.

American, possibly Ideal, twins, each 11.5", 1905 on. Shoe button eyes, short beige mohair, in very good condition. *Playthings* magazine, 1907, displays this bear being marketed through New York retailers. The thin parallel arms and pointed toes are marks of American bears. One of the promotionals for the company states "DeRigeur" (the fashion).
Value: Pair, $400-$600.

Antique Bear Pricing

Prices reflect actual sales by dealers and auction houses for the past five years.

American, Knickerbocker, 17", 1925. Between a wheel toy and American teddy of 1910.
  Value: Knickerbocker, $125-$250; American teddy, $100-$175.

American, Ideal, 1935-40. Left: 17″, glass-eyed with coarse, long cotton/mohair blend plush. Short mohair shaven nose. Good overall mohair content. Right: 18″ (musical). Near-mint condition. Glass eyes. Well set, overall countenance of this bear is collector-viable.

Value: Left, $185-$250. Right, $250 and up.

American, Ideal, 23.5″. This magnificent mint Ideal Bruin is almost identical to the Michtom bear found in the basement of the Smithsonian Institution. It is unfortunate that the bear is hidden from the public but may be viewed on request. This light-gold shaved-mohair bear has stickpin glass eyes and deep-set ears. In this condition his value is exemplary, for few have ever been sighted.

Value: $650-$1,200.

English Bears

CHAD VALLEY

Chad Valley bears are classic examples of English toymaking. Created from fine-quality mohair in beautiful natural and rainbow colors, these bears have been popularly priced for decades. Examples of this "bear from Birmingham" regularly turn up at sales because of their great numbers and wide distribution pattern.

To date, few Chad Valleys have reached the striking prices of the most desirable German bears; but these bright English bruins, with their unique kaleidoscope of mohair hues, are an absolute necessity for a well-balanced collection.

1823—founded as a family printing and bookbinding company in Birmingham, England, by Anthony Bunn-Johnson.

1919—product line expanded to include soft toys, dolls, and games; name was changed to Chad Valley.

1920s—Chad Valley expanded by purchasing other toy companies; began labeling all bears—to the delight of today's collectors!

1938—Chad Valley appointed "toymakers to the queen."

1950—Chad Valley became a public company.

1978—Chad Valley purchased by Palitoy, subsidiary of General Mills.

Chad Valley Clan, 28, 10, and 20 inches. These display the most recognizable of English features.

CHILTERN

The Chiltern teddy bear is quite different from any other English bear. Although it exhibits the same velveteen or canvas paw pads found in his Anglo brothers, there is an exceptionally soft touch to the mohair. An almost silky sensation is derived from the sweet-faced Chiltern.

The short feet and wide head proclaim his British bloodlines, but the overall design of this pretty bruin makes it easy to identify and separate from the average English bear. Some Chilterns were made in extremely large sizes, such as 38-40″. In 1986 a 40″ bear was offered at an antique show in New Haven, Connecticut, for $1,500, but it remained unsold.

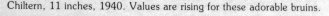

Chiltern, 11 inches, 1940. Values are rising for these adorable bruins.

1920—founded by H. G. Stone and Leon Rees in London.
1922—the company created a baby bruin.
1924—brand name "Chiltern" registered.
1947—the "Hugmee Bear" was designed.
1967—company purchased by Chad Valley.

DEAN'S

Dean's Rag Book Co. Ltd. was founded in London in 1903 by Samuel Dean. Its 1910 trademark shows two dogs tugging for possession of one of its cloth books. These washable, durable books ("for children who wear their food and eat their clothes") were part of a line of soft toys that included printed cloth dolls sold as kits for home assembly. Teddy bears were an early favorite in the Dean's line, and they patented a unique joint called "Evripose" that allowed the bears unlimited positioning.

In the 1920s Dean's began making bears and other animals on wheels

Dean's 13-inch Rag Book Bear. Note tags on feet.

and in the 1930s a series of named animals based on cartoon or storybook characters (Peter Rabbit, Mickey and Minnie Mouse, Dismal Desmond, etc.). By the end of World War II soft toys that included teddy bears, golliwogs, and other animals became Dean's main products. In 1972 Dean's Rag Book Co. merged with Dean's Childsplay Toys and purchased Gwent Toys of South Wales.

J. K. FARNELL

The pioneering English company of J. K. Farnell (c. 1840-1968) claimed, along with others, to have made the first teddy bear. It was developed as part of a series of rabbit-skin animals that were marketed in various countries, including Germany, where—according to one story—they inspired Margarete Steiff.

Alpha Farnell teddies, 38 and 24 inches, 1925-1930s.

One of the founders of the company was Agnes Farnell, sister of J. K. Farnell, and it was her creative genius, along with that of animal designer Sybil Kemp, that was responsible for such Farnell favorites as "The Alpha Bears." When A. A. Milne went to Harrod's department store in London to buy a toy bear for his little boy Christopher, it is thought that he purchased a Farnell bear, which Christopher named "Pooh." The rest is history!

MERRYTHOUGHT

Merrythought of England has produced some of the most entertaining and whimsical teddies in the world since its founding in 1930 by former employees of Chad Valley and J. K. Farnell in partnership with Holmes, Laxton & Co. spinning mills. The smiling expression and childlike eyes of the Merrythought bears make them very popular in the collectibles market, even though the earliest ones are scarcely in the semiantique category yet.

The first Merrythought line in 1931 was designed by Florence Atwood, who learned the craft while attending the Deaf and Dumb School in Manchester. A classmate of hers was the daughter of a Merrythought founder. Florence Atwood served as chief designer for the company until her death in 1949. Customer and employee satisfaction are high on Merrythought's priority list; a number of their employees have worked their entire careers with the company. A high quality of English knitted plush, an imported woven plush, and felt and fur are the materials from which Merrythought animals are constructed—still almost entirely by hand. Most of its production is sold within the United Kingdom.

Two Merrythought specialty bears, 1928 and 1930.

ENGLISH BEAR PRICES

English, Chad Valley, 17", 1935 on. Blue mohair with all tags present. Excellent condition. All original. Some fading of violet blue color. Unusual in color and condition.

Value: $500-$1,000.

English, Chiltern, 14". Treated canvas pads may be replacements in this classically English fellow. Glass eyes and original nose complement the ribbon he wore when he was bought in 1940 by an American naval officer.

Value: $250-$450.

English, Chiltern, 24", 1925. Gold mohair in excellent condition. Velveteen pads. Long cylindrical nose and beautiful expression are hallmarks of this finely sheared bruin.

Value: $350-$500.

English. Left. 20". Right. 17". Left bear is possibly English, 1920s, with dark gold mohair features similar to "Delicatessen," Peter Bull's "Brideshead Revisited bear." The bear on the right is probably "Alfa Farnell," 1915 on. He somewhat resembles Christopher Robin's "Winnie the Pooh" bear. His unfortunate hair loss certainly colored his sale price in 1985.
Value: Left, $350-$500. Right, $200-$350.

Antique Bear Pricing

Prices reflect actual sales by dealers and auction houses for the past five years.

English, Twyford, 12", 1930. Glass-eyed. Excellent condition. Velveteen pads. All jointed. Mark on back of left leg: Twyford, England. Clothing additional.

Value: (U.S.) $125-$175. (U.K.) $250-$300.

England, Twyford, 15", 1940 on. Good condition. Mohair has some wear in this lovely English Valley bear. He is beige and has a coarse wool mixed in with his mohair. His eyes are lovely dark glass. Clothes are additional.

Value: $125-$175.

In 1989 a similar bear with tag was sold at Brimfield for $150.

English, Twyford, 20", 1915. This happy teddy is missing 40% of his woolly mohair. His glass eyes and mohair are original. Pads are in great shape; nevertheless, his value will be seriously diminished by his hair loss.
Value: $175-$350.

Merrythought, 16", 1931, blonde mohair. Shoe button eyes. Black sewn nose with vertical stitches. Mouth and paws original, with webbed stitching on paws. Excellent condition. Purchased in 1988 for $1,100 (U.S.).
Value: $1,200-$1,500.

Chad Valley, clown, 16", 1920. Multicolored, gold, pink, and blue. Glass eyes, black vertical sewn nose, flannel pads. Purchased in 1985 for $475.
Value: $1,000-$1,500.

Merrythought, 15", 1930. Shoe button eyes. Black sewn nose. Cloth pads with Merrythought label (woven in silk thread). Celluloid-covered metal button with wishbone, left side of back.

Value: $650-$800.

German Bears

GEBRÜDER BING

Close-up of Bing button "GBN."

The brothers Bing, Ignaz and Adolf, founded their toy company in Nuremberg, Germany, in 1865. Their first products included tin and kitchenware and enameled toys. By the 1890s Gebrüder Bing was making toy boats, cars, and mechanical animals. Today Bing's early walking-tumbling bears are highly prized by collectors. Many of the bears were assembled and dressed by workers in the cottage industry, and it is probable that most of the colorful silk and felt costumes worn by Bing bears were made by such workers. Bing identified its bear with the mark "G.B.N." (until 1919) and "B.W." after 1920.

GEBRÜDER HERMANN

Johann Hermann and his children began to manufacture teddy bears in 1907 near Sonneberg, Germany. Sonneberg became a world center of toy manufacturing, where important American purchasers (such as Woolworth, Kresge, Borgfeldt, Louis Wolf, etc.) maintained offices.

Gebrüder Hermann relied somewhat on the handwork of the cottage industry and was one of the first toy manufacturers to encourage this kind of independent labor. In the early years a cottage worker would fill a basket

Majestic Hermann teddy bear, 25 inches, a rare and bullish bear, 1940.

with his finished toys, and the baskets would be picked up by the company on a regular schedule; the worker did not have to leave his home.

In 1948 Gebrüder Hermann moved its headquarters to Hirschaid near Bamberg. Teddy bears continue to be their top-selling product. Early Hermann bears are true collectors' items. Unfortunately, they did not have permanent markers and can be somewhat difficult to identify.

SCHUCO

In 1912 Heinrich Muller and Heinrich Schreyer founded the toy company in Nuremberg, Germany, that would go on to produce ingenious miniature

Schuco non-mechanical bear, 24 inches.

and mechanical bears for nearly half a century. The company name Schuco comes from an abbreviated form of Schreyer and Company. At the end of World War I, Schreyer left the partnership; Muller found a new partner in Adolf Kahn, and the firm began to produce a variety of novelty toys with intriguing mechanical designs. Today the Schuco Yes/No Bear (the head nods when the tail is moved), the Perfume Bear (whose head is the top of a perfume bottle), the Compact Bear (whose body opens to reveal a mirror), and various walking and tumbling bears are prized by collectors. The company ceased operations in 1970.

STEIFF

The Steiff toy company (officially Margarete Steiff, GmbH) of Giengen-on-the-Brenz, Germany, played a unique role in the development of the teddy bear and other stuffed toys. The story begins with its founder—yes, there really was a Margarete Steiff—who overcame daunting physical handicaps to initiate and lead her company for more than thirty years.

Margarete Steiff, born in 1847 in Giengen, contracted polio at 18 months of age. It paralyzed all but her left hand and arm. She would never walk, never marry. Nevertheless, Margarete was a cheerful and high-spirited child, who was pulled to school in a little wagon and entered into childhood games. She also went to the local sewing school, where, in spite of her seriously weakened right hand, she became adept at many kinds of needlework. She even learned to play the zither and earned money by teaching others. By the time she was 25, she had a thriving dressmaking business; and when she was 30 she opened her own small factory and hired a few employees to help her make fine wool felt clothing.

She made her first stuffed toy in 1879 from a pattern she found in the German fashion magazine *Modenwelt*. She gave the little felt elephants stuffed with lambswool as gifts, but they were so popular that she made more to sell. By 1883, her price list showed several sizes of felt elephants for sale as children's toys.

In 1883 Margarete's brother Fritz encouraged her to display the elephants at an export showroom in Stuttgart. She received many orders as a result of this enterprise, and Fritz then helped her make plans for a factory building and an expanded menagerie of stuffed animals.

By 1893 the first of Fritz's six sons—Richard Steiff—came from his art studies to work with his Aunt "Gretel" in the prospering business and was soon designing most of the animals. Within a few years his brothers Paul, Franz, Otto, and Hugo also joined the firm. Their youthful energy and

A rare black plushed covered bear, by Steiff, c. 1908-1910, $2,000-$3,500. *Photo courtesy of Christie's South Kensington.*

specialized training in various aspects of production and design—combined with Margarete's creativity and perseverance—were to place Steiff in the front ranks of the German toy industry.

Steiff's first stuffed toy—the elephant—was the work of Margarete; but its first jointed bear (the prototype for Teddy Bears) was the inspiration of Richard Steiff. According to Steiff archives, the company was making stuffed, non-jointed bears as early as 1892. By 1899 its catalog offered polar bears, dancing bears with handlers, and "Roly Poly" bears on rocking platforms. In 1902 a series of animals, including bears, was made with movable joints. The limbs were simply attached to the body by string. The animal shapes seem to have come from Richard Steiff's sketch pad, but it is not known who first thought of the jointed limbs. It was certainly Richard who devised the method used, however. When Richard's brother Paul carried the new toys to the United States early in 1903, he met with disappointment. The bear was obviously too hard, heavy and large ($21\frac{1}{2}$") for the American toy buyers. Margarete herself had feared the bear was too high priced to sell well.

In March of 1903 Paul showed the same bear—known as Bear 55 PB—at the Leipzig toy fair, again with little success. Then, as he packed his crates to return home, fate stepped in. Hermann Berg, a buyer for George Borgfeldt & Co. in New York, saw and fell in love with Bear 55 PB. He ordered 3,000 of them immediately. (One of the great unsolved bear mysteries today is that not a single one of these bears has ever been positively identified—and even the prototype is absent from the Steiff archives, although a dim photograph exists.)

In 1904 a smaller model of the jointed bear was displayed at the World's Fair in St. Louis, where it won a gold medal for its makers—and orders for 12,000 by the end of the year.

It was in November of 1904 that the Steiff button-in-ear trademark was devised by Franz Steiff. Until that time, Steiff products had carried a cardboard label marked with the company's logo of an elephant with an up-raised, S-shaped trunk. It is interesting to note that it is the motto "button in ear" that was given the German patent on May 13, 1905, not the button itself.

It was apparently a coincidence that Steiff began to produce the popular jointed bear at precisely the same moment in history when the teddy bear craze was sweeping America (following the November 1902 cartoon of President Theodore Roosevelt and the bear cub). Steiff built on the demand for their toy by aggressively advertising "the original teddy bear series." Their application for copyright of the name "teddy" and "teddy-bear" was denied, however (as was an application for a growler voice box); and many other companies in Germany and elsewhere competed with them for the bear market. The competition was exacerbated in 1907 by large orders being suddenly cancelled during a deep but short recession in the United States.

Ingenuity—as well as quality—kept Steiff in the forefront of the teddy bear business: Teddy B (for black or brown) and Teddy G (for gray or grizzly), based on Seymour Eaton's *Roosevelt Bears* books, were produced from 1907, wearing a variety of stylish clothes. Steiff's publicity department seems to have invented the story about President Roosevelt's daughter Alice using teddy bears as decorations at her wedding.

Margarete Steiff died in 1909 at the age of 62, leaving her nephews and nieces as owners/managers of the prospering company that bears her name.

During the next twenty years Steiff continued to develop new lines of toys and dolls, including some truly original items: the "Roloplan," an air and wind toy that was part kite and part glider; a plush chimpanzee radiator cap and a felt "Michelin Man"; animals with snap-off limbs. The Steiff factory was allowed to produce only war supplies during World War I, but by the mid-twenties was expanding again with the installation of conveyer belts and modern machinery.

In 1933 Hitler came to power. His policies hit hard at the entire German toy industry. The Nazis decided the competent women employees were needed for more important work. In the next ten years Steiff was forced to make war goods under the management of Hitler appointees. The few remaining toys were made of inferior substitute materials. In 1943 toy production was ordered stopped altogether and the efficient factory with its light-friendly glass walls became a munitions works.

Richard Steiff, whose genius had created the teddy bear, died in 1939 in the United States, where he had lived since 1923 as representative of the firm and developer of its outstanding production and advertising methods.

Miraculously, Steiff's archival material, which included crates of proto-type toys, production documents, and other treasures, escaped the rup-tures of the war and post-war periods, and today provide both a museum display and a historic record of the firm.

Not until 1947 was Steiff allowed to make a public offering of toys again. But since then, Steiff has regularly introduced new toys to a world-wide market and today also does a thriving business in reproducing, from its original patterns, teddy bears and other toys for the collector.

Its motto continues to be the words of Margarete Steiff, the remarkable founder, who wrote in her 1902-03 catalog: "For children only the best is good enough."

1904—Elephant buttoned teddy bear; Bärle or four-legged all jointed bear. The first Steiff teddy bear was named "Bärle" and when x-rayed exhibits rods from shoulder to shoulder and hip to hip; horizontal seam from ear to ear—shoe-button eyes and sealing wax nose; some Steiff elephants have been found to have the same rods. All have the early Steiff elephant button trademark.

1907—*Hot Water Bottle Bear* (1907-14). Stomach opened by lace hooks. A metal water bottle could be inserted and slept with on cold winter eves. Only 90 bears were produced because of lack of interest.

1908—*Muzzle Bears*. Novelties of 1908. Colors: white, brown, dark brown, 10 sizes.

1908—*Snap On Bear*. Limbs snapped on and off a teddy bear's torso. Only one example exists in the Steiff archives and it is actually a Golliwog with fastened arms and legs.

1908—*Polar Bear*, with coil neck and jointed limbs. Very popular, pro-duced in 6, 7, 9, 11, and 14".

1909 — Somersaulting Bear, "Purzel Bar." Examples have been found with shoe button and glass eyes. Clockwork mechanism works when arms are wound.

1909 — Roly Poly Bear. Came in four sizes, 7, 8, 10, and 14".

1910-18 — Marionette Bear - "Phantom-Bear," 14" and 16", less than 6,200 produced.

1910-18. 14" and 16"; only 6,268 were manufactured, shoe button eyes and horizontal nose brainchild of Albert Schlopsnies for Steiff.

1912 — Black mohair bear "sealskin,"* 1,214 produced, "mohair," 495 produced.

1913 on — Bar Dolly (1913-16) was a clown bear with wool ruff and body a colored mohair. The head was always white. They had "Hugmi" squeeze boxes and came in red, green, and yellow; 3 sizes, 10", 12", and 13". Just over 6,000 manufactured; no known complete examples have been sold in the United States.

1913 — Teddy Record, 1913 on. Three sizes, 4, 8, and 10".

1919-20 — Rough Wood Fiber Teddy Bear, 1919-1921. Made in five sizes, 13". 19,556 were made. Few have survived due to a most delicate fabric quality. Steiff also manufactured a bear on wheels made of nettle plants. This tweed-like bear was named *Brennessel-Bar* and is one of the rarest bears; usually 12".

1925 — "Teddy bu" or Teddy Boy. Made in four sizes; also came with a trousseau, which included brush, comb, umbrella, glasses, clothing, even pajamas.

1925 — 1925-26 "Tali-Bear" or Cyclist Bear (6,541 example).

1926 — Teddy Clown. Brown white-tipped bear w/clown's ruff and hat 11 sizes; 9 to 45". Also pink and gold. *1928 —* 30,000 made; several colors and tipped mohair; 5,271 yellow mohaired clowns made; 4,794 pink bears (1925-30).

1927 — Buschy. With wired ears and blue eyes, became Petsy the bear baby. Two versions; one brown-eyed, one blue-eyed; both 14".

1927 — Four patterns were made for head design; all apparently with center seam. Large, posable ears; some had red noses 6-20". Also available in hand puppet and "record" style. 10,668 were made to *1930*.

1928 — Petsy.

1929 — Teddy Baby. Blue mohair; 12".

1930 — Teddy Baby. With open laughing mouth; 5".

1930 — Teddy Bear. With wool plush; 17".

---

*Sealskin mohair (black) with gray tipping.

1930—Teddy Bear. With wool plush with open mouth; 12".

*1930—*Twenty-one displays of Teddy Baby at home were sold. Teddy Babies were also available as hand puppets. He was a great hit and considered a somewhat comic bear cub. He was made until 1950s.

1930—"Dicky." Happy face and unusual painted pads on feet; a "fascinating model." One of the most elusive of teddy bears, made between 1930-36; 14,646 were made in gold, only 11,029 made in white. A tea cozy which was Dicky-inspired was made around 1930. Possibly "jungbar" bear cub on all fours was also Dicky related. In Europe collectors have heard of "Dicky," but none has ever been offered at auction in Europe or the United States. Although production was comparable to "Petsy," for some reason this bear remains elusive to the market and therefore valuation is speculative. It is possible that a "Dicky" may well be one of the rarest Steiff bears of this decade despite comparable production. The list of unusual Steiff bears grows each year as the company unearths new archivial information (a snap-joint Dicky, 10"). Although production in the thousands seems grand, the limited production of 10 to 12 thousand bears will usually create a rare and most desirable market. In the past years many small and medium clown bears and Petsys have been found, including a few 30" examples of each. In America, only two Dicky's have been seen by the public and they are of the gold color measuring 14". They were not for sale.

*1934-35—*Steiff creates new numbering system. Prior to this year bears were measured in sitting position, now the entire animal would be measured.

1935—Circus Bear; 13" snap joints. Many positions.

1935—Teddy Bear. With dark brown mohair with red collar.

1938—"Panda" Bear. 12"; 1293 created in 1941.

*1938—*Fully bendable wool unjointed bear; 955 examples made.

*1939—*6"; 145 sold from 1951. Available in six sizes; 6"-20" remained in production until 1960s.

1940—Teddy Baby. In artificial silk mohair; 12".

1950-51—Turbo Bear. 5-6"; wore red vest and bow tie, tumbled.

1953—50th Anniversary Bear—"Jackie." A miniature 3" Jackie has once been seen, and three special order 36"-58" were seen in N.Y.C. parade. Very desirable bear.

1953—Nimrod Bear. Hunter bear; 9".

1964—"Zooby" Bear.

1967—"Cosy" Bear.

1969—"Minki Zotty."

1970—"Toldi." With apron.

1971—Toddel-bar in dralon.
1976—Teddy Zotty. Imitation mink with sponge filling.
1980—Dormey Bar. 14".
1980—Orsi. 12".
1980—Molly. 22", 26".

GERMAN BEAR PRICES

Bing (Gebrüder), 1910 on mechanical tumblers-mechanical (2) tumbler, August 1989. 12" and 14", white (left) and caramel (right). Both bears are in excellent condition and display the seldom seen but highly prized Bing side button. A slight resemblance to Steiff bears and early Hermann marks these classically German bruins. A 10" was sold June 1989 for $3,800 (U.K.); one sold at U.S. auction in July for $1,000 (mint condition).

Value: $1,200-$3,500 for each.

Hermann, "Teddy Baby," 9", 1960, honey mohair. Chain attached to plastic nose and orange collar. Air-brushed mouth and claws on feet. Glass eyes, mint chest tag (gold medallion attached to chest by red string).
Value: $700-$1,000.

Hermann, 18", 1930, honey gold mohair. Large "snout"; brown sewn, shaved nose. Horizontal stitches. Three claws. Growler not functioning. Felt pads excellent.

Value: $300-$500.

Hermann, 15", 1950, tan gold mohair. Glass eyes have distinctive orange and black as opposed to the medium light brown color of Steiff glass eyes. Note nose stitching, shape of nose and mouth. Hermann heads are usually broader with wider eye sets than similar-size Steiffs.

Value: $300–$600.

Hermann, 6", 1950, honey gold mohair. Glass eyes. Brown sewn nose with vertical stitching. Thread mouth and claws. Two additional outfits.
Value: $300-$750.

Antique Bear Pricing

Prices reflect actual sales by dealers and auction houses for the past five years.

Hermann, 20″, 1940. These two bears are made of acrylic fiber and some wool or cotton. Matting has set in, and the overall appearance is now shaggy. The cheaper version of these bears came unjointed and was used as a carnival prize, thus the name "Carnival Bears."
Value: Jointed, $150-$250. Unjointed, $50-$75.

Left. Hermann, 22″, 1940. Right. Steiff, 1984. Beautiful brown Hermann sits beside his German rival, Anniversary Papa Bear, by Steiff.
Value: Left, $450-$600. Right, $600-$1,000.

Left. Hermann, 24", mint. Right. Hermann, 15", 1935-45. Left: Glass eyes. Tipped-mohair Zotty lookalike teddy with closed mouth. Right: Medium Hermann. A most popular size. Excellent condition. Glass eyes. *Value: Left, $350-$450. Right, $275-$350.*

Hermann, 26", 1935, beige and gold. Glass eyes. All original with clothing. Glasses are a later addition. This bear has the typical Hermann shaved muzzle and large elongated feet found in German bears.

Value: $450–$750.

Schuco, "Professor bear," 1925. Yes/no mechanism and professor glasses, all in excellent condition. Sold in 1975 for $350.
Value: $500-$1,000.

Schuco, "Panda," 2.5", 1925. This metal-eyed miniature was passed down from a mom to her two daughters and then to a family friend. Mother was born 1920.

Value: $250-$275.

Schuco, yes/no bellhop, 9.5", 1923. Golden mohair (head, hands, and tail). Schuco patent tag on chest in particularly untouched condition. Shoe button eyes. Red and black felt outfit. No mohair exists under the suit. Tail is activator to yes/no head movement. Pink rayon pads. Original. All mint. Exceptional.

Value: $2,000-$3,000.

Schuco, yes/no, 14″, 1938-48. Mint in box, extremely rare. Various little "tricky" animals and some puppets are pictured on the box. Original ribbon on neck. Squeaker in belly. Some "tricky" bears also have music box in belly along with the yes/no mechanism. All functional in this bear. The later version of this bear is more popular than the 1920s issue.
Value: $2,000-$3,000.

Schuco, yes/no "Trickys," 8", 13.5", 20.5", 1948. All mint with Tricky plastic labels intact. Back of battery casement reads: Thorens #3065 Switzerland Music Box.

Value: Group $4,000-$6,000.

Antique Bear Pricing

Prices reflect actual sales by dealers and auction houses for the past five years.

Schuco Tumblers, 1940-60. Left: 5″, pale gold, glass eyes. Key-wind mechanism. Schuco Key #2. Center: 3.75″, Bellhop tumbler, gold head. Black metal eyes. Metal body. Key-wind mechanism on left side. Right: 4.75″, #1 Schuco key-wind. Blue and red felt outfit.
Value: Left, $500-$800. Right, $800-$1,500.

Schuco, Janus (two-faced) miniatures, 1955. Left: 3.75″. Light gold metal-bodied. Right: 3.75″, dark gold. Back view also applies to bear on left. Plastic tongue, metal nose, and plastiform ringlets in back of metal eyes. Excellent condition. Both bears were purchased in 1985 for $700 each at Cohen's New York auction.
Value: Prices still range downward from $800.

The bears are only moderately scarce, but the value remains stable.

Schuco, Perfume, 5", 1928-35. Mint condition. Gold. This bear usually turns up several times each year at doll shows and auctions. A good-condition early Schuco can realize $500-$800 to the collector seeking to complete his Germany "Gimmick" and mechanical collection.
Value: $500-$700.

Schuco, 1940 on. Group of multicolored miniatures. Note the dissimilar faces on the larger bears. All eyes are metal rivets, and bodies are metal cylinders clipped with tongue and groove fasteners. These little fellows hold up well over the years and often appear to be much more contemporary than they actually are.

Value: $150-$350 each (rare colors);
$125-$250 each (common colors).

Schuco, rollerskater, 8", 1935-40. This optimistic athlete has barely 30% of his original mohair but does have his original German rollerskates. Pads, nose, mouth nicely replaced.
   Value: $125-$175; in original condition, $450-$650.

Steiff, muzzled teddy, 1908, 13″. Note collar embossed with squared upper caps "Steiff," blank rivet at center of forenose. Shoe button eyes, short gold mohair in excellent condition. Some slight moth damage on forehead. *Value: $2,500–$3,500.*

Steiff, display bear, 5.5", c. 1948 (U.S. war zone Germany). All original tags and labels present. Excellent mohair throughout. All jointed with original threads on mouth and nose. Pictured beside a young girl measuring 5′ 4″. Investment potential: Six of these bears have been sold in the U.S. and in Europe in the last five years. The range of value has been quite extensive, and the last one to sell went for $2,400 at Sotheby's, London, 1986, from the author's collection. This bear failed to sell at auction, and negotiations after the sale resulted in Steiff of Germany purchasing the bear for a special room and exhibit in their museum. Two similar bears were sold in the $1,200-$1,500 price range, and prior to the Sotheby's auction one identical bear, missing both his button and chest tag, sold for $8,500 in 1985. It is clear that the potential for investment is great for large display items and that hidden values such as the fact that this bear is actually considered a logo bear for the Steiff Co. can create tremendous opportunities to bank on. In some cases such toys may appear on the market after the first one sells for a large sum. Only then will similar models surface, and the price usually drops accordingly. This bear represents a wonderful potential investment even for the beginning collector.

Value: $5,000-$8,500.

Steiff, teddy-record, 8", 1913 on. Bellows below seat. Legs have been disconnected.

Value: $2,500-$3,000.

Antique Bear Pricing

Prices reflect actual sales by dealers and auction houses for the past five years.

Steiff, 18″, 1905-07, pure white mohair. Excellent condition. This bear marked the highest price paid for a stuffed toy in 1983 at Withington's Auction Gallery, Concord, NH. He was an auction "extra," uncataloged, and in an auction that disallowed left bids and reserves, all these factors worked in favor of the lucky buyer. The blank button overlooked at preview time was certainly icing on the cake! Author's collection.

Value: $1,500-$2,500.

Steiff, 23", 1910-15, gold/caramel, medium-short mohair. 95% condition. Shoe button eyes. All original pads, etc.
Value: $2,000-$3,000.

Steiff, bear on wheels, 24" (1904-05). Excellent condition. Rich chocolate brown mohair. Blank button. An unusually dark, thick volume to the mohair, this bear is a scarce example of a pre-teddy (see previous page).
Value: $700-$1,000.

Steiff, 22"; Ideal, 22", 1904. Both Golden bears are from 1904-07; one from German stock, the other American. Note the difference in head positions and football-like torsos. These classic examples are top ambassadors of quality stitchery and workmanship. The American bear has very closely cropped mohair, and the Steiff has average-length German cut.
Value: $2,500-$3,500 each.

Steiff, 18″, 1910, canary yellow. 85% mohair present. Purchased in 1988 from private Pennsylvania dealer for $750.
Value: $1,000.

Steiff, 22", 1904-05, pure white. Blank button. Mint. Steiff unplayed-with purchased in 1985 for $300 from Pennsylvania dealer.
Value: $5,000-$7,000.

Steiff, white, 28", 1915-25, with button. 65-75% mohair present. White mohair, glass eyes, original pads, some important distress occurs throughout this bear. His patchy covering is accentuated by a bright white canvas backing.

Value: $2,500-$3,500.

Steiff, Teddy Baby, 3¹/₂", 1940-50. Excellent condition, features unusually symmetrical; all buttons, tags, accessories present and in mint condition.

Value: $750-$1,200.

Note: A collector's fantasy, this perfect "mini" Teddy Baby displays all the points the advanced bear and Steiff collector dream of. The collar holds five pressed brass buttons and original bell, and 1940s chest tag (note logo); even the paper is apparently untouched. *From Sarah Phillips's collection.*

Steiff, 14", teddy doll (or possibly eskimo doll, 1908-1919), rare. Not pictured. Mint condition (bear's body all jointed with doll's felt and mohair head).

Value: $2,500.

Steiff, matching white 13" teddy bear, excellent condition.

Value: $2,700.

Steiff, clown bears, 12", c. 1926. Mint condition. Tipped beige to brown mohair.

Value: $1,200-$2,500 each.

Note: The clown bear is exceptionally appealing to many collectors and is only rarely found with both original ruff and poled hat. These two appear to be Pierrot and Pierrette, and when sold as a pair would escalate in price considerably. Steiff Co. items were found in every imaginable size and larger display pieces were easily custom-ordered. The Steiff clown bear has been found in sizes 7", 9", 10", 12", 15", 19", 22", 24", 28", 30" and 45". An allowance should be expected of roughly $100 per inch, with additional value allotted for all original accessories and mint condition. In 1984 one mint 7" Steiff clown bear was sold (privately) for $700, and in 1986 a 28" one lacking its hat and ruff but with 95% mohair present sold for $2,500 (Mass.). These bears may be confused with the similar "petsy" bear.

Steiff, deep rust red elephant buttoned mechanical "circus bear," 16". Although this bear can be seated and appear exactly like his teddy bear brothers, he was actually manufactured to portray a bear on all fours. This is the first true teddy bear created since his button bears the elephant insignia that was instituted in 1904-05 by Steiff. Roughly 15 of these bears have crossed my path in the last 8 years, ranging from 15" to 30". Many of these bears were beige, two were white, one was red and one gold. One caramel bear was 22″. One 30″ mint white circus bear is privately owned, and the owner cannot assign a value to him. It is likely he is one of the most desirable bears in the world to date.

Value: 16″ circus bear (rare red color) $2,500-$5,500
(allow less for beige/gold).
Mint condition: $6,000-$10,000.

Steiff, miniature Teddy Baby, 3″, 1940. Mint condition. Brown with chest tag and button over ear tag. Original buttoned collar and brass bell also present. Comments: This pristine little charmer is rare and much sought after. His price per inch far exceeds that of any other miniature Steiff teddy bear (nonmechanical). His larger brothers are often available for the same or for a fraction of his price.

Value: Good condition: $450-$1,000.
Excellent condition: $1,200 and up.

Steiff, mini "Teddy Baby" group, 3", 1929-50. Here we see the four distinct colors of Steiff from left: white, dark brown, gold, caramel. Note the smallish head on the second from right, signifying one of the very first "Teddy Babies."

Value: $450-$1,000.

Antique Bear Pricing

Prices reflect actual sales by dealers and auction houses for the past five years.

Steiff, 7", c. 1910, beige/gold "humanoid." This very individual teddy has similar proportions to humans and balances a very small head compared to his bruin brothers. He is extremely rare and desirable, and in his case is in extraordinary condition. Left: 9" white Steiff. Right: 7" "humanoid." *Value: $700-$1,500.*

Skittles (bowling pins), 1892 to 1900. Eight in all—cat, rabbit, monkey, bear (king), dog, curly dog, elephant, jackrabbit.

Value: $10,000-$15,000.

Marionette teddy bear, "Phantom Bär," 12", 1910-18. All joints hang from threads instead of being "pinned" to discs, etc. Strings are gone, but bear is in excellent condition.

Value: $2,500-$4,500.

Steiff, display facade, late 1940s on. This 7' animated village display made for Hutzlers Bros. store was put up every Christmas in the window of their Howard Street, Baltimore, store. Part of this display was attached by means of a rod that extended to the center and held three teddy bears washing clothes. Very few of these displays remain intact because of easy separation. This piece has marvelous investment potential. This display sold in 1988 in the U.S. to a West Coast collector.

Value: As entire display in excellent condition:
$15,000-$20,000 and up if complete.

More Bears

This miscellaneous section is comprised of bears which have only partial identification or known origins. More information is needed in the future to predict the stable market prices for these bears. Many have surfaced in the same countries or carry reliable past histories so that some assumptions have been made, and, as clearer references are provided, the mysteries of these interlopers will dissipate.

German, Polish, Steiff, and large American bears with the usual range of white to dark brown mohair are found internationally. The colors seen here might be classified white, cream, beige, caramel, orange, deep gold, gold cinnamon, brown, red brown, rust red, and faded gold.

A collection of 23 similar bears may well be valued at around $50,000 in America by today's world values. The same collection would probably bring more than $100,000 in Europe if 1988-89 values are enlisted. Of this collection 50.05% was sold between 1986 and 1988, for a total of more than $30,000.

MISCELLANEOUS BEAR PRICES

German, 2-faced bear. Bisque faced doll on back of bear's head. All jointed. Sold in 1985 for $1,800. NY auction.
Value: $2,500-$3,500.

Antique Bear Pricing

Prices reflect actual sales by dealers and auction houses for the past five years.

Polish or Swiss, 21″, 1940, white mohair (angora). Center seam, extra-large gold glass eyes, large snout, brown sewn nose, mint felt pads. *Value: $1,000-$2,500.*

Swiss mutzli, two 8.5" honey mohair boy/girl pair, 1960. Glass eyes, vertical black stitching on nose. Girl, mutzli tag on chest. Red check pinafore. Bow, silver beads original to bear. Boy, 8.5", mutzli button in ear. Blue and white check pants, white felt collar.
Value: $275-$500 each.

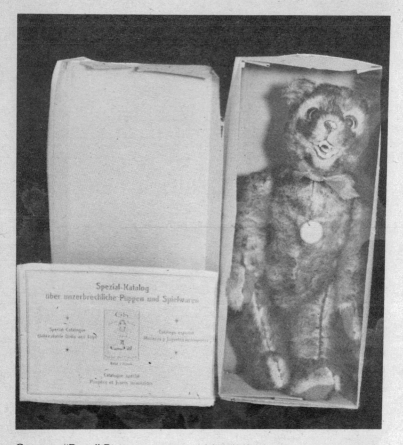

German, "Peter" Bear, rare, approx. 14", 1925. Original organdy ribbons (red). Glass eyes. Original tags on bodies read: "Peter, Geo. Gesch. (legally protected Nr. 895257)." Fully jointed, swivel neck. Head is *hollow* and holds eyes that move side to side as the tongue moves in the open mouth. Molded papier-mâché mouth and teeth, hard papier-mâché nose. Original box with original label has picture of Peter and reads: "Neuheit Bar Wei Leband." Translation: "Novelty Bear, most nature-like finish." Made in factory Gebruder Susserguth in Neustadt near Coburg, Thuringia, Germany. Brown tipped mohair with golden beige base near body.

Value: $2,500-$4,000.

French? musical bear, 15″, 1920. 65-75% white mohair with bluish tint, glass eyes. Original nose, claws, paw pads. Probably was clown with hat and pom-poms down front of chest. All missing now.
Value: $600-$1,200.

Polish? 28", 1915-25. Angora mohair, long-faced teddy. Clothes are additional. Pads in good shape. Beautiful endearing expression is a quick draw to many collectors. This unusual and much sought-after bear is a collector's dream find.

Value: $1,500-$2,000.

Polish, 35", 1925 on. The glorious dense quality of his tresses marks the immediate marketability of this sensational bruin; 100% angora mohair. All excellent condition. White (rare).

Value: $3,000-$3,500.

Polish, 17", 1925 on, light gold (canary yellow) angora mohair. This bear was retrieved from a Polish garbage can in 1953 by an American army wife. Twice former owners have tried to buy him back because of his inordinate and magical countenance.

   Note: It has a straight nose top-line.

Value: $1,000-$1,500.

German, unknown, 28", 1907-10. Golden mohair, Gulliver-like features make this bear rare and extremely desirable. He has extremely long arms, huge hockey stick feet, thick short mohair, and original pads, threads, and shoe button eyes. (Collar is a recent addition.) This unusual teddy is an example of the unknown selling for an exceptional amount due to condition.

Value: $2,000-$3,000.

Antique Bear Pricing

Prices reflect actual sales by dealers and auction houses for the past five years.

Left. Possibly Schuco, 22". Right. American, possibly Ideal. Beautiful tipped or frosted mohair is usual to the German group of fine bruins. In some cases, German bears resemble their competitive manufacturers' examples. Very few still wear labels, and points such as eyeglass color, foot shape, and classic head form per company are the only hallmarks of particular makers.

Value: Left, $250-$350. Right, $250-$350.

American, bear twins, 28", 1907 on, sold through American retailers, possibly German imports. Excellent condition is more than evident on the pads and in the eyes of these bears. The standing bear has shoe button eyes, possibly replaced. Sitting bruin has glass eyes, more often found in these beautiful display pieces. Larger bears, especially of American origin, were found as mascots and promotionals for bakeries, pharmacies, and dry goods—or as apothecary items. In some cases they might have been imported from Germany and marketed by American companies. The distinctive noses on these toys may someday be recognized and identified.
Value: Left, $1,000-$1,500. Right, $1,000-$1,500.

Unknown, 15", 18", 1925-35. Light yellow. Glass eyes, felt pads. Nose stitching on left bear is seen with German Clements, but no label or similar model has been seen with definite provenance. Bear on right resembles Swiss bear with mechanical music box or rocker mechanism (growler). *Left, $150-$200. Right, $150-$250.*

Unknown. Left. 14", 1905. Right. 16", 1935 on. Left: Dark gold short mohair. Original pads, shoe button eyes. Nose, original. Round putter-like feet found in early German bears. Beautiful all-around condition (ribbon not original). Right: Two-toned mohair, glass eyes. Footless features similar to English bears and some Swiss. No marks.

Value: Left, $450-$650. Right, $250-$350.

Possibly Japanese, 2.5″, 1930s. Rust, cotton plush/wool blend. Sewn eyes, nose, mouth, duo jointed limbs—each limb movement brings the corresponding limb into the same position. Some repair to seams. Dress not original. Purchased in 1986 for $35.

Value: $85-$100.

Left. Possibly English, 14", 1930s. Center. German (Hermann), 24", 1930. Right. Japan, 17", 1930. Left bear is of cotton. Maker unknown. Center bear is acrylic plush. Unknown company. Bear on right is also acrylic plush. Unknown company

Value: Left, $125-$150. Center, $175-$250. Right, $150-$200.

Non-Teddy Bears

This section of the book is dedicated to all the pre-teddy toys on up to current unjointed and mechanical novelties. It is included here so that the contrast with the jointed, soft stuffed teddies in other chapters may be more readily appreciated. In most cases the bears on the following pages are much scarcer than the wonderful creatures inhabiting the rest of this book.

Antique Bear Pricing

Prices reflect actual sales by dealers and auction houses for the past five years.

NON-TEDDY BEAR PRICES

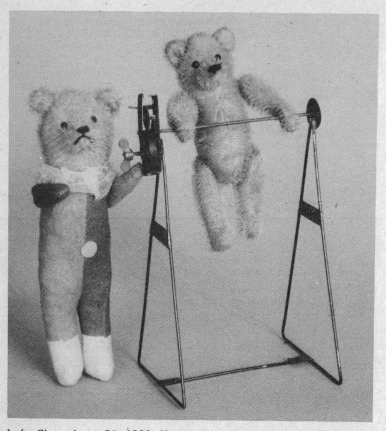

Left. Clown bear, 9", 1920. Unjointed, gold mohair head, glass eyes, black sewn nose and mouth, red/blue felt pin jointed arms. Red/blue felt body. Yellow felt feet. Gauze ruff. "Germany" stamped on left foot.
Value: $200-$250.

Right. Germany, bear with trapeze, 7", early 1900s. Gold bristle mohair. Rigid head, black bead eyes, black sewn nose. Trapeze measuring 8.25" high by 5" wide. Key-wind clockwork mechanism.
Value: $650-$1,000.

Possibly English, 13″, 1920s-1930s. Beige mohair (head, paws, feet).
Red plush body, yellow plush legs. Three brass buttons, black bow tie.
Squeeze tummy and mouth opens to reveal red felt mouth.
Value: $250-$350.

Germany, Japan, 1920-40. These bears are all non-teddies and were sold for a range of $150-$450. The scooter bears have a clockwork mechanism that was still functional.

Value: Bears on all fours: $150-$450.
Scooter bears: $275-$350 each.

Japan, marked L & R, 1925 on; left, 4½"; right 6". Tricycle bell toy is unusual tin with clockwork mechanism. Roly Poly is similar in features to Schuco toys. However, stitching in seams is wider and less detailed. Metal eyes. Maché body with polychromed gesso marked "Japan" on bottom. *From the Trusdell collection.*

Value: Left, $150-$200. Right, $250-$450.

Germany, mechanical (non-teddy), 4', 1920s. This all-original mechanical display retains his original history on paper. Mechanism is working (electrical). Shoe button eyes and stitched nose all excellent. Wool over maché armature.

Value: $800-$1,200.

Steiff, unjointed "Teddy Baby," Tyrolean suit, 9", 1948. Tan mohair muzzle, glass eyes, black sewn nose, open felt mouth, jointed head, extremities, wire armature, nonjointed. Linen body and pads. Red felt jacket, white blouse, black felt pants. Raised script button and U.S. zone, Germany tag (right leg).

Value: $750-$1,000.

Carnival type (possibly Swiss), duo jointed, 12", 1930. Immobile head. Ears are cut into the head, fitted into slits. Shoe button eyes. Single pin joint crossed inside torso from shoulder to shoulder, hip to hip. When one appendage is mobilized, the corresponding part also moves. Some of these bears came from Japan, c. 1920.

Value: $85-$150.

Steiff bear on wheels, 10", 1907, ginger-colored mohair. Double F underscored button in left ear. Shoe button eyes. Jointed neck. Squeaker functioning.

Value: $950-$1,200.

Company unknown, bear muff, 1920. Brown mohair, jointed head.
Value: $500-$750.

Company unknown, glass eyes. Black sewn mouth. Nose and claws. Pillow-stitched stationary arms and legs. Cloth lining (linen brown). Purchased in 1986 for $450.
Value: $450-$850.

Schuco Soccer Team (11), 3.75", 1938. Beige mohair, headed, wired mini-bears. Beige pipe cleaner arms and legs. Metal button eyes. Black sewn nose and mouth. Dressed in various felt colored uniforms. Shoes marked *7800/16 HEGI* (Group of 11).

Value: $2,000-$3,000.

Antique Bear Pricing

Prices reflect actual sales by dealers and auction houses for the past five years.

This 30″ tall, mint white Steiff was wrapped in tissue since 1910 until its sale in 1986.

Roosevelt The Laughing Bear. Possible prototype for one with wood jaws. *From the Port Collection. Photo by John Paul Port.*

Left. A 1945 vintage, 10″ Schuco, "yes/no" panda.
Right. A 20″ white 1903 Steiff.

All photos, unless otherwise noted, are by Carol-Lynn Rössel Waugh.

"Jonathan," 18″ tall, was made of golden tan mohair by Christine Shelters. His lady friend is a 14″, 1907 gold mohair Steiff.

The 28″, two-toned white Steiff bear with glass eyes wears a vintage "mourning locket." His companion is a 19″ tall, "center seam" distressed mohair bear by Barbara Conley.

Left. A 1926-1929 unjointed white Steiff bear with glass eyes. *Right.* Nona Pebworth's mohair teddy, "Aunt Emma," made in 1989, wearing a Victorian doll's nightshirt.

"Jenny-Lynn," © 1988 Carol-Lynn Rössel Waugh, 21½" tall, wears a pale pink bridal gown. Her "groom" is a 20" tall white Steiff bear. Popcorn heart by Eric-Jon Rössel Waugh.

A 16" tall Steiff (1889 Elephant button) and Beverly Port's 12" tall, gold mohair bear inspect a reproduction antique train engine.

Left to right. A 1920s, 11″, gold mohair Steiff, 7″ off-white mohair "Goobear," © 1989 Carol-Lynn Rössel Waugh, and 1907 gold mohair Steiff.

The 24″ Steiff on the left brought a world record price in 1984. Dolores Grosseck's 20″ tall lady bear wears a mauve and black winter ensemble.

A 1903 Steiff bear made of silky mohair. "Button," by Bonnie Windell, and Steve Schutt's dark gold 6″ teddy are ready for bed.

Left to right. Schuco 5″ bear, 1925-1935, 5″ Steiff, 1903, with a 3″ Steiff on top, 5″ mauve mohair bear by John Port, orange, short napped mohair teddy by Kimberlee Port.

The panda on the left, by Durae Allen, is 6″ tall. The Schuco mini panda, made in 1935, is 3″ tall. Both are mohair.

The light-brown, 14″ tall Steiff on the left, circa 1915-1920, courts Sandy Brazil's "ethnic" ragbear, who has a muslin body with mohair head and paws.

Left. An 11″ 1930s Steiff "Dickie" bear, of rare size and shade, and the only known example in North America. *Right.* A 12″ "Pee Wee Rosenbear," by Gloria Rosenbaum. It won a Golden Teddy Award in 1988.

Beach scene: a 14″ mint 1905 Steiff, 7½″ "Shoo" by Bonnie Windell, and 12″ white Steiff from 1903.

Left. Orange-red mohair, "blank button," 1903 Steiff teddy in unfaded condition. *Right.* A 22″ tall "Stier" bear, by Kathleen Wallace, made of distressed mohair.

Mohair "compact bears." *Left.* Durae Allen's 3½″ peach-colored bear, made in 1989. *Right.* A 1925 purple Schuco bear in excellent condition.

Modern Bears

"Guardian of the Fairy Folk," by
Brenda Dewey, is 26″ tall and made
of distressed mohair.

Made in 1989 of brown mohair, 12″
"Ma-wa-qua" (Little Bear), by Nancy
Crowe, wears a Great Lakes
trapper's "skin coat," with beadwork
by Rose M. DeLand.

"Queen Titania," © 1989 Beverly
Matteson Port, is a FabriArt™
Original made of imported cream-
color wool plush. She won a Golden
Teddy Award in 1989.

Germany, bear atomizer, 4", 1920s. Bright gold shorn mohair, totally un-jointed. Two small arms and legs. Bronze bottom unscrews. Mark incised: *DRPA DESETZUCH GESCHUTZP.* Press bellows in stomach and perfume is dispensed out of metal nose. Eyes are cut jet stone.

Value: $1,000-$2,000.

American carnival bear, 12", 1930. Totally unjointed. Dressed in original outfit with tiny mohair tail. Shoe button eyes. Black sewn nose and mouth (horizontal stitching). White felt collar, blue polka-dot shirt, blue felt pants; orange, black, and beige felt shoes.

Value: $250-$450.

Special Bears:
One Collector's Dream

Pat Volpe is the quintessential teddy bear collector. In the few years since she started collecting she has limited herself to the purchase of bears under 17 inches and generally in the category of miniature or small cabinet size bears.

Seven years ago Pat bought her first bear at the Amherst Teddy Bear Rally in Massachusetts. To date she has carefully selected over 300 bears, which form one of the finest miniature-to-cabinet-size American and European bear collections on the East Coast. Her keen sense of design and investment is evidenced in the variety and scope of her selections. Her husband, Jack, a businessman and investor, has been most supportive of her hobby, realizing the great investment potential of her furry friends. Recently, however, Jack has stated that they multiply much too quickly.

To Pat, the teddy bear is a constant symbol of love, friendship, and security. Her genius for selection has generated a faultless criteria and exemplary vision.

The bears included in this section are from the Volpe collection. Patricia and Jack are sharing, for the first time, a rare vision of one collector's ultimate dream.

SPECIALTY BEAR PRICES

Germany II (possibly), Strauss musical, c. 1910, beige mohair. Clear glass eyes with black pupils, rust-colored nose, vertical stitches, three claws, pads leather (red one). Back has porcelain-knobbed crank that is rotated clockwise to produce music. Rare mechanical.
Value: $2,000-$2,500.

Steiff twins, each 8-8.5", 1905. These perfectly white matched beauties were purchased from the O'Neils of Vermont, 1983. They bear full family provenance and were kept in impressive condition for 84 years. They each have shoe button eyes, brown sewn noses, horizontal felt pads on the feet only. Rare and very desirable couple.

Value for pair: $4,000-$5,000.

Antique Bear Pricing

Prices reflect actual sales by dealers and auction houses for the past five years.

Steiff, 14", 1905, pure white. Excellent pure white hue. Blank button. Brown stitched nose (horizontal stitches). All jointed. Felt pads in very good condition.

Value: $2,500-$4,500.

Note: This teddy bear holds the valentine that came with him in 1907, mailed 11:30 A.M. from Brooklyn, NY, Station B. His message reads: "Loves Telegram 'To My Valentine' Wire date can't wait. Be quick love sick. No joke. Heart broke." The sentiment and resulting provenance involved with this remarkable bear give him immense natural appeal, historical and otherwise.

American, electrical-eyed bear, 20", 1920. Red mohair (head, one ear, one arm, one leg). Dark blue mohair turned black. Bulb eyes operate by pushing button inside back. Black sewn nose and mouth jointed. Red and blue felt pads.

Value: $800-$1,500.

Germany, white mohair character-style bear, 7", c. 1930. Glass eyes, brown sewn nose (vertical stitching), open felt mouth. Head moves in circular motion when tail is pulled. Velveteen pads on paws and feet have a separation for big "thumb" or large "toe," respectively. Jointed arms. Gussetted fanny (unjointed hips). Extremely rare. The craftsmanship and structure are not dissimilar from "Bearskin," the wardrobe teddy. This bear has not been positively identified by Steiff; however, it has not been *vetoed* positively either. More research is underway. A mystery ted indeed!

Value: $2,000-$3,000.

Germany, 8" Bearkin, 1938 provenance (F.A.O. Schwarz Christmas Catalogue). Wardrobe of 10 pieces, including suitcase. Glass eyes, brown stitched nose, red stitched mouth, all jointed, squeaker operational. Mint condition all over. F.A.O. sticker on blue suitcase. Tyrolean pants, jacket, purse, two scarves, ski blouse, pants, cap, three skis, four poles. We have seen two of these sold in 5 years, both 8". There is definite proof of a waiting list for this little fellow. We have also noticed three 28" Bearkin-type bears apparently made by the same company, always extremely large.

Value: 8" with wardrobe: $2,000-$3,000.
28", no accessories: $2,500-$4,500.

Germany, probably Steiff, 16", 1905-10. Tan/gold mohair. Shoe button eyes. Black sewn nose, mouth, and three claws. All jointed. Felt pads excellent throughout. Very big feet!! Beautiful silky mohair and endearing expression enhance the value of this scrumptious bear.
Value: $1,500-$2,000.

Republic of Ireland, musical, 18″, 1949. Cloth tag on right foot. Gold mohair. Glass eyes, leather pads. Unusual nose stitching. No claws stitched on feet. Key-wind music box (on back), plays "Teddy Bear's Picnic."
Value: $350-$650.

Germany, Bing Tumbler, 10″, 1910. Shoe button eyes, black nose. Four claws, all jointed. Squeaker excellent. Linen original pads. Metal button left arm G.B.N. (Gebruder Bing, Nuremberg).
Value: $1,500-$2,000.

Germany, Bing Tumbler, 9″. All mint with crisp, unused clockwork mechanism. Beautiful dark chocolate mohair and mint outfit lining torso and bodice of bear. Shoe button eyes. Bing button on right wrist. In England during July 1989 a similar bear in chocolate brought £3,800. One week earlier this bear was purchased for $950 at an American country sale.
Value: $1,000-$2,000.

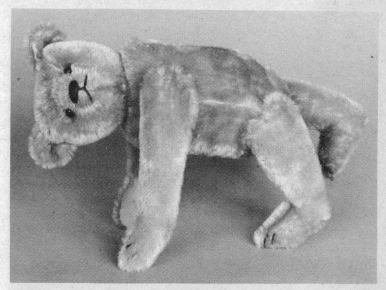

Steiff, Purzel Bär, Tumbler, 12″, 1909. This mint bear has no Steiff button, yet his exquisite quality is thoroughly commensurate with Steiff or Schuco. His head is identical to one found on a rare Steiff marionette in Maryland in 1986. He is honey gold with shoe button eyes. Black sewn nose. He has one rigid leg, which is probably a temporary condition. Arms perform clockwise. All systems functioning well otherwise.
Value: $2,000-$3,000.

Steiff, Muzzle bear, 1908, 13". Beige/gold mohair. Shoe button eyes. Jointed tilt squeaker. Felt pads. Double F imprinted on leather muzzle. A similar bear sold in U.K. for almost four times the price of this U.S.-purchased marvel.
Value: $2,000-$3,000.

Steiff, white "Muzzle," 16", c.1908. Mint throughout. Brown stitched nose, four claws, mint felt pads (except one). Double F underscored button in ear, on muzzle. Leather muzzle and leash came with this bear.
Value: $6,000-$10,000.

Steiff, twins, 7", pure white. Ear stitching on outer rim is an unusual feature. Brown stitched nose, glass eyes. Pewter button in left ear.
Value for pair: $2,000-$3,000.

Steiff, twins, 12", 1904 on. Honey mohair. Excellent throughout.
Value for pair: $4,000 and up (with provenence).

Steiff, 16", 1907, dark ginger. Mohair extra plump. "Grandpa bear." Huge feet, paws, extra-long nose, and thick waist mark this unmistakable bear.
Value: $2,500-$4,500.

Steiff, "Jackies." Left: 9″, all mint with deep 1954 original air-brushed colors; these colors usually wore off because they were the "frosting on the total toy" as seen in the larger and smaller versions. Center: 15″, excellent condition. Right: 6″, excellent. Note the all-important "white stitch" horizontal inset across black nose threads.

Value: Left, with literature, $3,500 and up.
Center, $2,000–$3,000.
Right, $800–$1,200.

Steiff, 9.5", 1905-25, silky plush. Dark gold. Shoe button eyes. Linen pads. Double F underscored button. Wonderful and unique facial structure of this bear extremely scarce.
Value: $2,000-$2,500.

Steiff, clown bear, 11", 1929. Frosted mohair, glass eyes. All jointed. Functioning squeaker. Felt pads mint. Hat and ruff original and mint. Double F underscored.

Value: $1,500–$2,500.

Schuco, bear on kiddie cart (record style), 14″, 1910. Mohair is brown pressed leather or sealing wax nose. Car measures 13.5″ (length) by 7.5″ (width). Four wood wheels, red wood seat. Bear is attached to the metal base. He moves up and down on the seat when toy is pulled.
Value: $1,500-$2,500.

Antique Bear Pricing

Prices reflect actual sales by dealers and auction houses for the past five years.

Unknown, musical clown, 13". White curly angora goatshair. Glass eyes, pink sewn nose. Squeeze box in stomach emits a Viennese waltz when "clapped" from front to back. Velveteen pads. White felt clown hat with two pink pom-poms.

Value: $1,000-$2,500.

Germany, Petz, 14", 1910-20, orange. Burnt tips to fur. Frosted brown, glass eyes. Squeaker mechanism in belly. Mint condition for this rich bright color.

Value: $1,500-$2,000.

Unknown, possibly "Anker," 11", 1960. Apricot, long mohair. Angora pile mohair on front of ears. Exposed canvas on back. Plastic eyes, open felt mouth with red felt tongue. Jointed head. Squeaker not functioning. Unjointed arms and legs.

Value: $150-$350.

Modern Bears

Carol-Lynn Rössel Waugh

Contemporary, Handmade
Teddy Bears:
Art, Craft, or Investment?

Are you prowling antique shops and boutiques, flea markets and sales, searching to replace the teddy bear you foolishly abandoned in adolescence? Do the paucity and prices of antiques make you growl? Take heart; the bear of your dreams may become reality.

The teddy bear market's character is rapidly changing. As old bears grow scarce and pricey, "designer teddies" are taking their place as today's hottest ursine collectible.

Except for age, these charming bruins sport the same desirable attributes as antiques: rarity, originality, and "name value," offering buyers the added bonus of "art patron" status.

Although artists have been quietly designing and making original bears since the early 1970s, awareness of their work has only recently reached the general public. Today's bear buyer has the luxury of a wide variety in style, size, materials, and price. The choices he must consider when purchasing teddies are at times confusing, which is why we have compiled this guide.

To evaluate today's ursine offerings intelligently, it is wise to discover whence they come. Compared with antiques, contemporary, handmade teddies were "born yesterday." But their roots stretch back almost a quarter of a century.

The first "art bears" were made by doll designers who made original teddy bears, selling them surreptitiously to discriminating doll collectors. The first "teddy bear artist" of record was Beverly Port, who was well known for her work in many art media, not only dolls, when she began exploring bears as an art form. The first showplace for "designer" bears was doll conventions. Artists tucked original teddies alongside dolls on sales tables, eliciting stares of disapproval from officials. When mixed-media bear/dolls entered competition, they routinely were disqualified. But they sold.

Starting on the northwest coast of the United States, largely because of the influence of Beverly Port's work and teaching, the movement spread south in the early 1970s, attracting craftspeople, artisans, and artists— perhaps because the area was affluent and probably because of its appreciation for and understanding of crafts, a legacy of California's many "flower children."

These dollmaker/bearmakers worked in a vacuum, often unaware that others shared their enthusiasm, and this isolation brought forth vailant efforts in original styling with make-do, hard-won materials.

Output ranged from copies of antiques to experiments in mixed media. The dollmaking background of many of these bearmakers gave them an advantage many contemporary bearmakers lack: a knowledge of traditional sculpting methods and construction techniques, an awareness of the history of dollmaking and dressmaking, and the know-how to apply these to their work.

By the late 1970s, bearmakers were becoming aware of the existence of peers, and the second wave of the movement began. Interest in teddy bears in general was simultaneously beginning to blossom, as early books on the subject by British authors such as Peter Bull (*The Teddy Bear Book*, 1969) and Margaret Hutchings (*The Book of the Teddy Bear*, 1964; now called *Teddy Bears and How to Make Them*, a pioneering teddy bear pattern book) piqued public consciousness.

Many of today's popular bear designers got their start reproducing Hutchings's designs. Those whose work proved meritorious learned basic techniques, soon developing distinctive, original styling and "artistic voice."

By 1980 the Teddy Bear Movement reached its third wave. Many more people jumped onto the teddy bandwagon. Shops began stocking and selling handmade bears. West coast bearmakers still predominated. However, quality was uneven; many craftsmen and artisans made teddies.

About this time I began research for a book called *Teddy Bear Artists: Romance of Making and Collecting Bears*, published in 1984 by Hobby House Press. For me, an art historian/doll artist turned teddy bear designer and working in isolation, it was an attempt to discover peers and to document their work.

The book required three years of exhaustive research because networking among bearmakers was nil. It offered in-depth profiles of more than fifty artists, in many media, using the teddy bear as subject matter. Most made plush bears.

Magazines and newsletters aimed at teddy bear lovers, such as *The Teddy Tribune*, *Teddy Bear and Friends*, and *Teddy Bear Review*, which began publishing about this time, highlighted handmade bears and their makers in articles and photo spreads.

By 1985, because of increasing awareness of the existence of "bear artists," coupled with the rising number of stores specializing in teddy bears, public demand for art bears exploded. The successes of the first three waves of bearmakers attracted still others, and the fourth wave began.

Quality and quantity improved, as did bearmaking supplies (and their availability), especially after the American Teddy Bear Artist Guild formed in 1985. Bearmakers started sharing sources, tips, problems, and leads and forging long-distance professional and personal bonds.

Teddy bear conventions and shows expanded in size and number to satisfy demands of both collectors and bearmakers, and the "bear show circuit" seemed at times like a "road show"—the cast of characters remaining roughly the same, only the location and merchandise changing with the passing months.

In about 1987 the fifth, and current, wave of bearmaking began, as craftspeople increasingly discovered the field and viewed it as lucrative. They began competing with established artisans for limited markets, forcing them to push their work to new limits.

Because of constant cross-pollination and commercial need to outdo last month's production, bears began to evolve rapidly as bearmakers experimented furiously with new materials, new concepts, new techniques. Their output began challenging the definition of what a teddy bear should be; some individuals produced work that crossed the borderline between craft and art.

In 1987, under the auspices of *Teddy Bear Review*, New York's Incorporated Gallery staged the first professional art exhibit of the work of "American Teddy Bear Artists," establishing prices commensurate with those of fine art objects. Since then, other galleries have showcased teddy bears as artwork, and select artists have increasingly commanded escalating prices, especially for one-of-a-kind pieces.

But are today's art bears art?

Sometimes. It depends on who makes them. And how they are made.

The term "teddy bear artist" is now liberally misapplied as a catchall term for anyone who hand-makes a bear. Similarly, handmade bears are often called "artist bears" because they are made by people calling themselves "bear artists."

Often, everyone using this term is incorrect.

Art is a process, a way of seeing the world, a special way of reinterpreting reality through ideas. One cannot just state that he or she is an artist; one must earn the right to be called an artist, and one does it by producing artwork.

It seems to me that for a bear to be an artist bear it has to be made by an artist, by someone with an inborn ability to see the world in artistic terms and to express that with a freshness of vision, technique, and concept. If one is lucky, one has years of training to hone those talents.

Usually, artists are facile in more than one medium and can transfer skills (perception, adeptness, insight) from one to another. They are able to see connections between unrelated items and ideas and bring them together with aplomb. They reject copywork and steer clear of timeworn concepts, of ideas already explored by others, seeking, instead, untrodden avenues of expression.

Most of all, a true artist is able, through his work, to *stir emotion* in his audience and make it see anew through his eyes.

The process of creating fine art is solitary. Commercial artists may, by the nature of their projects, have to do art by committee to target it to a marketplace or meet the requirements of clients.

Even when he has patrons, a fine artist works in isolation. His product is made by his hands alone, often emerging via a slow, intuitive, nonverbal trial-and-error process.

Sometimes such an individual creates teddy bears. Only then is the product an artist bear.

For a teddy bear, then, to be an art object, it must rise above the ordinary by inspired concept, by iconoclastic panache, through the emotive quality of its face. Luxurious overabundant clothing and accessories will never lift a mundane teddy above its origins.

And to my mind, for a teddy to be considered an artist bear it must be *completely* crafted by its artist/designer.

That is why artist bears are scarce.

On the other hand, finely crafted teddies made by artisans and craftspeople abound. A bear need not be art to warm the heart, and fragile rarities are hard to hug.

The bearmakers who create these charming bruins are often excellent technicians producing beautiful, well-made products with consistent quality. If the truth be told, some of the best-known bear designers and artists will never equal their superb execution and attention to quality control.

Their work comes in all sizes, shapes, colors, and permutations. Today's collector of handmade bears has heretofore unimaginable wealth to choose among, thanks in part to the competition necessary for today's bearmakers to "keep up."

This half of the book is a guide to buying contemporary handmade bears. It features descriptions and photographs of the work of 68 American bearmakers.

The way this work is produced varies greatly, and a single designer's involvement in the field may be on many levels. For uneducated buyers, this can lead to confusion; they may not be purchasing what they really want to.

For example, it is possible to buy a signed bear designed by a well-known, "established" artist but not possess a work of art, nor a bear that that artist has ever even seen. And yet, since no one has invented a teddy bear machine, this bear *is* "handmade" (how many hands have combined to make it is another question).

Only if the "artist" (if he is one) personally hand-makes the complete bear and its accoutrements is it an art bear. If the artist does not do that, than it is another entity entirely, even if he signs it.

The difference here, to use an artistic parallel, is that between a painting and a print. If an artist paints a portrait, it is his original work of art. If he then has either another person or company make a print of the painting (or even if he does it himself), this is a "reproduction" of the painting, even if it is signed by the artist.

Let me propose a scenario to make things a bit clearer.

1. Ms. Bear Artist, one of the most talented designers in the field, has decided to sell some of her original work. She hand-makes these bears entirely herself, and they are called "artist originals."

2. She finds she has more orders than she can handle, so she hires a seamstress to help her. The seamstress is so efficient that she can translate the artist's ideas and sketches to fabric, and she does all the work except for the faces. The artist finishes the faces to give the bears her own "look."

These bears are no longer originals although they are, in fact, original *designs*. They are collaborations and should bear not only the designer's name but that of her helper; they should be marked "designed by" followed by the artist's name. Because they are not completely made by the artist, they should *never* be sold as artist originals.

3. The artist finds orders are piling up and she needs more help. She hires more seamstresses, a couple of stuffers, someone to joint the bears, and a secretary. She still designs, makes prototypes, and supervises. Sometimes she even does faces. She now has a cottage industry and is a manufacturer. Her product is an artist-*designed* bear, never an artist

original. The size of her operation is not a factor in the title "manufacturer." Some well-known companies in America, and especially abroad, are quite small, relying on piecework done by homeworkers for the majority of their production.

4. The artist still has more ideas than she can handle, so she approaches a commercial manufacturer to reproduce her designs on a royalty basis. She provides this company with a handmade sample, called a prototype, and patterns, which the company replicates, as best it can, in a factory, probably in the Far East. (Many bears are made in South Korea because of the high quality plush and low wages available there.) The designer now probably has *no* control over her bear's production.

These teddies may carry her name and even her signature but may look nothing like her originals. They may please many people and reach a vast audience because of their low price point. They are *commercial designs by an artist/designer*, never artist bears.

❦

As time passes, will contemporary, handmade teddies increase in value? Some already have, especially work of early artists and of well-known people who no longer make bears.

It is difficult and foolish to predict any set rate of increase in the prices paid for work by contemporary artists and artisans. History and the marketplace will determine how their product is priced ten or fifty years from now.

Since we are dealing here with a product that is currently being produced under widely diverse circumstances, for different subaudiences under one collector canopy, it is unwise to predict whose work will be a good investment, if that is your goal.

The collector of contemporary handmade bears has, I believe, an advantage over the antique-bear collector. He can keep up to date on the latest trends and artisans through shows and trade magazines. He can compare and contrast work either by mail or in person, and he can specially commission work to meet his needs.

On the other hand, he is at a disadvantage if he wants a time-proven "sure bet." There aren't many. However, as in any field of collecting, there are basic guidelines to follow and things to look out for. The following suggestions should make bear hunting less risky.

The reputation of the bearmaker is a good starting point for making purchasing decisions. Many people seek out "name" bearmakers. However, newer, less established people also produce superb work, and these may just be the ones to watch. As in any field, a bearmaker's longevity often equates with quality, but only if his or her work is constantly evolving. One basic design in seventeen different colors, fabrics, and sizes, with new clothes and story lines every six months, does not qualify.

The contributions an artist has made to the field outside bearmaking add to his résumé, giving credibility and value to his work, as does professional recognition in terms of awards and commercial contracts.

The fewer bears an artist makes, the more valuable each one is. Thus, a bear made by a prolific artist (one who makes lots of bears) may not, down the road, have as much investment value as one by an artist with limited production. Of course, much depends on the bears in question. Outstanding design can override these parameters.

Is the bearmaker an innovator or a follower? Do his designs stand out because of appealing facial expression perhaps, or daring or innovative use of materials, techniques, or colors?

Upper-echelon teddy bear makers have recognizable, personal style. Like Seurat's pointillist dots or Van Gogh's brushstrokes, a bearmaker's "signature" shows in the way a nose is stitched, the way the eyes are set, in the bear's persona.

The best designers are daring, whimsical, outrageous, playing with new concepts, new fabrics; yet their personal style, their way of expressing the "teddy bear essence," shines through all of these experiments. The past may inspire them, but they use it in unexpected, offbeat ways, not reproducing or copying bears designed by others. (Why waste time with retreads when there are wonderful new things to make?) Usually, they do limited editions or one-of-a-kind designs.

In time (and today the time lag can be the few weeks between teddy bear shows), innovators are copied. Their ideas filter down as diluted ripoffs selling to the less discriminating.

The most desirable handmade bears are "all original," made entirely by the designer. Their freshness of concept, their flair, their fine workmanship set them apart.

Reputable bearmakers mark work "designed by" if they did not actually hand-make every part of it. If this is important to you, if you're paying for a bear to be "artist-made," ask.

Some "name" artists have begun designing for well-known toy companies in the United States and abroad. Their involvement varies, and hangtags should be checked to see to what extent the artist actually was involved in the development of the toy bearing his or her name. The involvement of some "celebrities" consists of lending a name to a product designed by in-house designers. Some provide sketches from which the product is made. This is *not* designing; it is merely offering inspiration.

Now that you have a whetted appetite and an idea of your prey, how can you track down these rare bears? Start looking at gift, specialty, and toy shops. Many now have a "stable" of bearmakers and are proud of the people whose work they have selected to represent. A knowledgeable owner can introduce bears by favorite artists, recommend books and magazines, even take special orders.

Look at "bear events": conventions, rallies, or sales. Here collectors can often meet bearmakers and compare work on the spot. The interaction with other arctophiles you'll experience at even one "bear rally" is invaluable, resulting in leads, solace, and inspiration. Word of new designers rockets through the bear world's extensive underground network. Become a part of it. Sharing the hunt is fun; it could be profitable.

Look in collector magazines such as *Teddy Bear Review* or *Teddy Bear and Friends* for up-to-date information on bearmakers, shows, supplies, and sales. Shops offering exclusive and limited-edition bears often advertise in such magazines, and they welcome phone calls and special orders.

But don't look for bargains. Although some cost under $100, teddies by "name artists," when available, can fetch well over $2,000.

Before making such an investment, ask yourself why you are buying this bear. For interior decoration? Status? Resale? Love? I hope your motive is the last.

If you fall in love with a bear, buy it. There will never be another exactly like it. Don't worry about resale; you're adopting a friend, not a portfolio.

Keep in mind that Teddy will likely remain with you for years. Look for a personality in tune with yours. Wait till he speaks to you, looks at you a special way, before picking him up. Whatever your aesthetic standards, sometimes the most technically imperfect bear, the silliest one on the shelf, will say "take me home." If this happens, follow your heart.

Otherwise, look for workmanship. Are the ears sewn on well? They should appear to grow out of the head. Are the seams finished, with no thread showing? Has the fur been brushed from seamlines? Is the design excellent, original? Is it signed? Is its face wonderful? Of what is it made? Today mohair is "status," promising durability, huggability, and a large price tag. Real fur is a poor choice, as it can disintegrate.

Once you've found a bearmaker whose work you admire, who captures the teddy bear essence exactly for you, ask if he or she does commissions or special orders and how long one might take. Share your dreams, your hopes, your memories. Just maybe, working together, you'll be able to approximate (but never replace) that love-worn teddy you stashed, and lost, so many years ago.

A BUYER'S CHECKLIST

Questions to consider before buying a handmade bear:

1. What is the reputation of the bearmaker, including contributions to the field? How long has he or she been making bears?
2. Is the design original?
3. How rare is the bear? The work of a prolific artist (one who makes many bears) will, in general, be less valuable than one with very limited production.
4. Is it well made?
5. Exactly who made the bear? Was it completely made and dressed by its designer?
6. Is it signed?
7. Is its face wonderful?
8. Am I in love?

How to Use
This Section

The 1990s may one day be remembered as the heyday of the American Teddy Bear Artist Movement. As the decade begins, handmade teddies abound and are being welcomed into households nationwide. To answer this perceived demand, hundreds of artists, artisans, and craftspeople in search of fame and fortune have threaded sewing machines, invested in mohair, and hung out shingles, dubbing themselves "teddy bear artists."

Faced with this proliferation of bearmakers, how does a collector develop an eye for quality, a nose for selecting work that will increase in value (if this is one's goal), either monetary or aesthetic? The only guideline I can recommend is familiarity with the field.

A serious collector should look at as many bears, good and bad, as he can, both in photographs and in person. He should read extensively, following trends and developments. He should use his eye and his instincts and, if all else fails, his heart. Eventually, this thorough immersion should, if one is diligent, result in developing a knack for spotting "good bears."

This process is slow and highly subjective. Because it is so personal, as is any aesthetic decision, the collector should base his purchases on his own taste and needs, not on those of "experts"; few exist in this field, and their taste may be different from one's own.

If you are a connoisseur of art bears, I hope this book will keep you up to date on today's trends. Much has happened since I wrote my first book on bear artists in 1984. Many talented, established bearmakers have gone on to produce gallery-caliber work, some of which has become desirable and pricey.

Perhaps the most important development in those half-dozen years is the explosion of excellent new artists and artisans offering vigor and fresh viewpoints.

If you are a fledgling collector, I hope this book will serve as an armchair companion, an introduction to the world of antique and contemporary bearmakers and designers. Here you will find inspiration, diversity in styles and prices, and a chance to make comparisons without leaving home. When you finally attend a show and see your first "designer teddy" in the plush, you and your purse will go prepared.

This is not an exhaustive, all-inclusive guide to every bearmaker active in America at press time. It offers a varied sampling of the work of 68 American teddy bear designers. Some are well known; others are beginners. Because of space and time limitations, many fine bearmakers were omitted.

Although this book is technically a price guide, it is extremely difficult, and perhaps unwise, to affix firm prices to the work of currently producing artists. Many rightly feel that their work—and their prices—are evolving.

I am therefore circumventing this controversy by listing for each bearmaker a *broad price range*, stating his highest and lowest suggested retail prices. Some work may fall below or above stated prices, and none of the bearmakers is bound to honor any quoted price range. These retail prices, obtained from the bearmakers or their agents, were current only at the time the book was compiled in late 1989. If you are reading this book in late 1990, prices will probably be higher than listed. These prices reflect only the general *retail selling price range as determined by the bearmaker in question*.

In the following section I describe the output of each bearmaker in a consistent, objective format. In the long run, this should be far more valuable to you, the consumer, than individual prices. I try to include factors such as the bearmaker's standing in and contributions to the field, how long he has made bears, his best known work, any innovations he may have brought forth, his style, and output. When possible, I indicate bearmakers who do all of their own work, those who have helpers, and those who have cottage industries. Some artists design for commercial toy companies, and I mention this when appropriate.

I asked most of the people participating in this book specific questions about their production and methods of working. Not everyone answered all of my queries; the responses I received varied enormously, both in completeness and timeliness, as did the quality and acceptability of photographs submitted.

I gave most coverage to those whose responses were substantial, whose photographs were excellent, and whose work is, in my opinion, significant. This is a subjective judgment based on my on familiarity with art bears since the movement began in the 1970s and on my training as an art historian.

These profiles are of necessity slanted toward the needs of the buyer, and I hope that, by making comparisons, you can make up your own mind as to the desirability and future collectibility of the work of not only the bearmakers shown here but, using these guidelines as a standard of comparison, the work of others.

In years to come, the prices here may be outdated, but because of the way it is structured, this book will still be a valuable tool. More important, it will serve as an historic record of the diversity of work produced through 1989 by contemporary American bearmakers.

Contemporary
American Bearmakers
(From A to Z)

DURAE ALLEN

❦

L'il Honeys By Durae

The close-set dark eyes and doleful expressions of Durae Allen's "L'il Honey" bears are her unmistakable hallmark. She began making them in 1984 after attending a teddy bear show and realizing the fun her mother, the late bearmaker Cappi Warnick, was having.

In college her major was theater arts, and she had extensive training in costume design, as well as practical experience in crafts. These talents are evident in the often theatrical ensembles and costuming she arranges for her bruins.

Early Allen bears were made from synthetics, but now they are chiefly crafted from German mohair, alpaca, and angora. Most are fully jointed, with glass eyes and hand-stitched noses. They range from 1 inch to 4 feet in height and are of two types: toys and "art pieces."

The toys are less expensive, more traditional teddies, made with children in mind. The art pieces are, at times, complex combinations of bears and paraphernalia: teddies on carousel horses, in swan boats, astride seahorses. These are meant to be displayed as sculpture and are geared for adults.

Durae works ten to twelve hours a day, seven days a week, filling orders, both retail and wholesale. She can finish a basic bear in two hours and can complete twenty bears a week. She displays her work at the New

"Elyssa on the Elephant Carousel" by Durae Allen. The carousel measures 20 inches tall. The elephant is made of silver-gray mohair fabric and has brown glass eyes, swivel neck, open mouth and a bendable wired trunk; 10-inch tall Elyssa is crafted of pale pink alpaca fabric. *Photo by Carol-Lynn Rössel Waugh.*

York Toy Fair (which gives her enough orders for the year) and at shows throughout the country.

Because orders became so overwhelming, in 1988 she arranged to have some of her designs produced in Germany. The manufacturer does everything but the faces and perhaps some of the final finishing; these Durae does herself.

Value: "L'il Honeys by Durae" range in price from $50 to $500.

This open-mouth teddy by Durae Allen is made of pink alpaca with white wool felt paw pads. She is fully jointed, with sparkling blue glass eyes and a mauve hand-stitched nose. She wears a bright blue bow on her leather collar. *Photo by Carol-Lynn Rössel Waugh.*

MAGGIE ANDERSON

❧

Anderson Originals

A dozen of Maggie Anderson's tiny teddy bears can easily fit inside a matchbox, and yet each is full of whimsy and beans.

Maggie is proud of her artisan membership in the International Guild of Miniature Artisans and has worked in an arm's length list of job descriptions in the art field. She taught herself to crochet, working from afghans (boring) to full-scale "fantasy toys" from her children's drawings.

Maggie's micro-bears began around 1974, when she was asked by a miniature enthusiast to successively reduce a normal-size bear she had crocheted. By the time it had shrunk to ³/₄ inch and was a hit, Maggie knew she was in business.

Using a No. 13 crochet hook and sewing thread, the New Hampshire resident crochets angel bears, Indian bears with loincloths, bears with bal-

"Ice Cream Cone Bears" by Maggie Anderson, 1 inch and ³/₄ inch tall, respectively, toting crocheted ice cream cones. Each requires the same number of stitches; size is determined by thread use. *Photo by Carol-Lynn Rössel Waugh.*

loons, merbears, Edwardian bears, blue-jeaned bears, and baby bears with bibs, ranging in size from ³/₄ inch to 2 inches.

Besides bears, she crochets rocking horses, possums, alligators, mice, and other creatures. When time permits, she does special requests. Limited editions, such as the "Statue of Lib-bear-ty," which is on permanent display at the museum on Liberty Island, are about $25.

Maggie's tiny teddies have found their way into dollhouses within dollhouses and into several museum collections. At times she makes them into jewelry, and they become wearable art.

"On a good day I can do ten bears," she says. "Figure out my annual production from that."

Each requires approximately 500 stitches, and size is determined by the thread Maggie uses, which may even be of antique fibers she hoards for special occasions.

Anderson Originals are available from select shops, at shows, and by direct mail.

Value: They range in price from $8.50 to $65.

CELIA BAHAM

❦

Celia's Teddies

"Sheldon in Roosevelt Suit" by Celia Baham is 21 inches tall. His head, hands, and feet are made of mohair; his suit and legs, of old army blankets; his leggings, of upholstery fabric. He is fully jointed with nuts and bolts and has glass eyes and gold wire eyeglasses. *Photo courtesy of Celia Baham.*

Native Californian Celia Baham was taught to sew at an early age by her mother, who was a sample seamstress for the garment industry. An artist in several media, she combines her skills to translate flat drawings into three dimensions.

Celia began making stuffed toys more than twenty years ago, when her children were young, but she began making and selling collector teddies around 1983. She is perhaps best known for her elegantly trimmed one-of-a-kind carousel bears astride white felt horses, one of which was optioned for commercial production by Enesco.

Celia's fully jointed glass-eyed teddies range in size from 1 ½ inches to 24 inches and are usually made of mohair or sometimes from wonderful old coats. "I can get seven bears from a coat if I'm lucky," she says. "This nicely limits the edition." Often she combines fabrics for special effects.

A favorite of the more than two dozen designs in her repertoire is Sheldon because he dresses so well. Most of Celia's teddies are dressed. "The Victorian era influences my costumes, especially when I'm decorating the hats," she says. Most are for collectors. Once in a while Celia designs special sturdy ones for children.

Working a half day, six days a week, Celia makes 75 to 100 bears annually. "When my orders got larger, I hired a gal to do some sewing for me," she says, "but I found her personality got into the designs and made them different from what the customer ordered. Now I do all the work." Most bears are limited by fabric availability, but some, like Sheldon, for whom she won a Golden Teddy award, are unlimited.

Celia's Teddies may be bought directly from shops or at shows.

Value: They range in price from $60 to $600.

LINDA BECKMAN

❦

In 1986, after designing hand-painted muslin dolls, Linda Beckman purchased a teddy bear pattern, but it didn't fit her image of a proper bear, and she began pursuing the elusive perfect bear.

"Elisabeth" by Linda Beckman is 20 inches tall, made from tan distressed mohair. She wears a print dress, vintage collar, pantaloons, and slip. *Photo by Carol-Lynn Rössel Waugh.*

"It is such a joy to create bears," she says, "but it is also fraught with frustration, discouragement, and much intensity. Only recently have my bears begun to emerge as my mind envisioned them. Can you imagine how badly a prototype must feel to have someone look into her eyes and tell her she is just not right? I usually cover my new bear's ears and speak softly so she will not hear the truth."

Linda's distinctive bears, with sweet smiles, range in size from 7 1/2 to 23 inches and are almost exclusively mohair. They have glass eyes and wool pads and are fully jointed. Arms and legs are long, and torsos are slim, with a nipped-in waist at the back, a humped back, and rounded bottom. Her bears have a round-point snout, reminiscent of early Steiffs, or a more traditional face with a shorter, more square snout.

She uses needle-sculpting techniques to give each bear a special look and takes great care with both the interior and exterior to produce a fine product. "Stitching a perfect nose is just so crucial to the bear it seems to take forever," she says.

Most bears are one of a kind and costumed in Victorian or country-style clothing featuring trimmed and flounced underskirts, pantaloons, and accessories. Linda designs and makes each bear herself. They are readily identifiable by the hand-signed tag stitched into the left foot.

Annual production, which may be purchased from select shops or directly from the bearmaker, is limited to perhaps 100.

Value: Linda Beckman's bears range in price from $125 to $475.

JO-ANN BLAIR-ADAMS

"Mr. Curly White" by Jo-Ann Blair-Adams is 19 inches tall and made of antique angora mohair. *Photo courtesy of Jo-Ann Blair-Adams.*

Jo-Ann Blair-Adams attended the Rhode Island School of Design, majoring in apparel design and illustration. She graduated with a BFA in 1972.

A collector of old plush animals, especially dogs, Jo-Ann combined her love of animal forms and fabrics to create her own soft toys in the mid-1970s. Around 1982 she began making teddy bears.

Although they have a nostalgic look, these bears were more of a fiber artist's interpretation of the old ones she loved than reproductions. Using old fabrics almost exclusively, when Jo-Ann started, she wanted to combine a sense of antiquity with that of being an artist, perhaps to create three-dimensional fabric sculptures.

Often she finds inspiration for her pieces from the fabric itself, which is cleaned, reconditioned, and occasionally hand-dyed. This results in one-of-a-kind work. Size (12 and 19 inches) and a uniform pattern, developed years ago, give her work unity.

"I don't do editions," she says, "and I've totally stopped counting how many I've made." With the birth of her second child, she fell into semi-retirement, and today she makes very few teddies, perhaps two dozen a year. Most are bare.

"I don't dress them, except maybe in antique clothes," she says. "I'm a bearmaker, not a dressmaker, and I'd rather spend time on the bear's face."

They all sport small white identifying labels in an arm seam and are available at Grrreat Bears in Baltimore or by mail order.

Value: Blair-Adams bears range in price from $45 to $250.

SANDY BRAZIL

"Creativity has always been an important part of my life," says Sandy Brazil. "It is part of who I am as a spiritual person." Today the Minnesota resident divides her time between making teddy bears and acting as spiritual companion while she pursues a master's degree in counseling psychology.

She began making teddies around 1980, learning construction techniques from books and making do with materials, but they were a hobby until 1986, when she began to work in mohair.

"Katrina the Little Folk Dancer" by Sandy Brazil is a 16-inch-tall "ragbear." She has a jointed mohair head, mohair hands, and muslin body. Katrina's costume is made of both new and vintage fabrics and trims. *Photo courtesy of Sandy Brazil.*

"Sara," named by Sandy Brazil for her daughter, is a 14-inch-tall "ragbear" with a jointed mohair head, mohair hands, and muslin body. Her dress is made from an 1890s doll dress pattern. *Photo courtesy of Sandy Brazil.*

Sandy is perhaps best known for her beautifully dressed "rag bears," who often wear ethnic costumes, and she traces their birth to a love for floppy dolls.

"My daughter loved Raggedy Ann," she says, "and I still remember the cute positions I'd find 'Raggedy' posed in when she had been abandoned for something else. I love dressing my 'rag bears' and try to give them an old-fashioned look. I use vintage trims as often as I can and feel a sense of connection and gratitude about the life of some unknown person who worked with her hands to create something pretty like a dresser scarf trimmed with hand-done embroidery and crochet. It gives me a warm feeling to know that her work will be enjoyed in a new way by someone else."

Sandy's bears range in size from 5 to 16 inches tall and have either jointed mohair bodies or floppy muslin ones. They have charming, gentle expressions that mirror their creator's feelings about her work.

"For me," she says, "there is something mystical about teddy bears. Sometimes I look up, and a bear is just sitting there quietly looking at me as if it were able to look deep into my soul in a very accepting and loving way. Creating teddy bears is a very contemplative part of my life. It helps me to stay centered. Life is filled with pain as well as joy, and I believe a special teddy bear companion made with tender loving care can help us celebrate our joy and comfort us in our pain."

Sandy's bears are available by direct mail, from The Owl and the Pussycat in Ft. Myers, Florida, or Gambucci's in Hibbing, Minnesota.

Value: They range in price from $65 to $200.

REGINA BROCK

Regina Brock studied art at the Cleveland Museum of Art, Kent State University, and the University of Akron, specializing in graphic design. From the start she has approached bearmaking from the point of view of

Linen-bodied mohair bears by Regina Brock. The larger bear is 14 inches tall; the smaller is 10½ inches. Both have conventionally constructed bodies of raw linen. All of the mohair on them is sewn in by hand, using a needle and small amounts of mohair roving. They are fully jointed, with glass eyes, felt paws, and embroidered noses, mouths, and claws. *Photo by Paul's Photographic Studio.*

a sculptor and a fiber artist. And her techniques differ radically from the norm.

When she decided to make mohair teddies in 1981, mohair yardgoods were not readily available in Ohio. But Regina knew that was the only material suitable for her work because of its softness and durability. So she experimented endlessly with the raw fiber, which comes from the soft underbelly of angora goats. In its unprocessed state it is called "mohair rovings."

Finally, after many failures, she devised a means of "sculpting" the rovings, which she first hand-dyes, into a three-dimensional form. She creates a skeleton armature of wire, nuts, and bolts and sews the mohair fibers into a layer of padding around it, strand by strand, "building" the fur around the glass eyes of the face to hold them firmly in place.

This painstaking process takes approximately twenty hours and results in a bear 3 to 6 1/2 inches tall. But she cannot work continuously on a bear; artistic judgments about length and width and size happen with each needle insertion. And the procedure is mentally and emotionally tiring.

Because of this, each bear is unique. Scale in the small bears is excellent because the fibers are fine; no backing exists to show through and jar the illusion of reality. There is also no stuffing; the bears consist of armature, glass eyes, felt paw pads, and mohair.

In 1985 Regina's bears grew to 12, 14, and 16 inches, and once again, she used atypical techniques.

To achieve the larger size without the weight of a metal armature, Regina constructed a fully jointed bear underbody of linen. Into this she sewed, strand by strand, hand-dyed mohair rovings. This technique is a bit like constructing a three-dimensional hand-hooked mohair teddy bear "rug." It is done very slowly with fine sensitivity and an artist's eye.

Regina regards her bears as art pieces, not as children's toys, and markets them as such. They are a remarkable combination of nostalgia and invention and have a gentle, old-fashioned elegance in their bearing and facial expression.

She produces forty or fewer bears a year, working on commission from her Ohio studio, where she also uses the above method to restore threadbare elderly teddies.

Value: Regina Brock bears range in price from $275 to $2,000. *

---

*See Antique Bear section for more on Regina Brock.

LYNDA H. BUCKNER

The Incredible Teddy®

"The Wedding Party" by Lynda Buckner includes a 12-inch bride and groom, 8-inch ring bearer, and flower girl. The bride wears antique lace and taffeta with pearl accents; the groom wears black velvet. The boy, wearing blue velvet, carries a white satin pillow with ring attached. The girl wears pink taffeta and carries a satin-covered basket. All are fully jointed, made of light brown mohair, and have glass eyes. *Photo by Carig's Photography.*

Lynda Buckner of Niceville, in the Florida panhandle, was a doll artist for five years before beginning, in 1983, her line of original teddy bears under the banner of "The Incredible Teddy"®.

Lynda learned to sew at the age of five on a treadle machine, and her needlework expertise is reflected in the finely detailed custom clothing many of her award-winning bears wear. Special surprise touches include, at times, earrings and shoes.

Her line is diverse, as are her materials, which include antique quilts as well as fine imported mohair and alpaca. She also makes an autograph bear, a favorite of teenagers.

Buckner bears range in size from 7-inch-tall "Bitsy Bears" to 28-inch character bears made to suit each customer's fancy and special needs.

Value: "The Incredible Teddy"® ranges in price from $75 to $295.

JANE CARLSON

Kenja Designs

"Molly" by Jane Carlson is 18 inches tall and made of beige mohair. She wears a print pinafore over complementary print dress and panties, shoes, stockings, and bow. She is limited to 25. *Photo courtesy of Jane Carlson.*

Jane Carlson has devoted most of her life to sewing, starting with doll clothing at the age of seven. A home economics and fashion merchandising major in college, she ran a fabric store, designed and made clothing for men and women, and went on to create soft sculpture dolls.

In 1984, after making dolls for ten years, she branched into teddies, combining soft-sculpture dollmaking and dressing techniques to produce unusual, readily recognizable rosy-cheeked "bear dolls."

These well-dressed cubs made of velour and vellux often sport corkscrew curls and handmade shoes and range between 4 1/2 and 11 inches. Although they are her designs, Jane now just needle-sculpts the faces on most of them; they are done by subcontractors on a piecework basis.

"Andy" and "Ashley" by Jane Carlson are 12-inch-tall needle-sculpted teddy dolls made of vellux. *Photo courtesy of Jane Carlson.*

But she completely constructs and dresses her larger mohair bears (9, 15, and 18 inches tall). These well-dressed, fully jointed little girls, which debuted in 1987, often come with trunks of clothes and teddies of their own.

"I don't think all bears should be dressed," she says, "but because of my background in clothes design and dolls, my bears seem naked without clothes."

The Arizona dollmaker has made as many as 1,000 and as few as 350 bears in a year. Many are limited editions. Current annual production is approximately 150.

Kenja Designs are available directly from the artist.

Value: They range in price from $35 to $500.

CAROL CAVALLARO

❧

Taddy Bears

Carol Cavallaro of Madison, Connecticut, makes bears from 6 to 24 inches tall; her most popular range from 8 to 15 inches. They are often made from mohair stuffed with polyester or pellets, are fully jointed, and have glass eyes.

"Freesia," "Lily," and "Clover" by Carol Cavallaro. "Freesia," made of white mohair with Ultrasuède paw pads, is 15 inches tall. "Lily" is 9½ inches tall, is made of gold mohair, and filled with pellets. "Clover" is approximately 10½ inches tall and made of brown matted mohair. *Photo courtesy of Carol Cavallaro.*

She began making bears around 1984 when her mother entered a nursing home and needed a "friend."

"Teddy bear making," she said in 1989, "has been my most important interest for about five years. Love for teddy bears began for me many years ago when I was a small child. My first real friend, the kind you can really, really trust, was a teddy bear.

"As most people know, teddy bears never tell a secret, and as a child being adopted by a single person, 'Pooh' and I had a lot to talk about. I have had a soft spot for bears ever since."

Carol's bears are not limited editions. "It depends on how creative I feel," she says. She sells by direct mail, at shows on the east coast, and through select stores.

Value: "Taddy Bears" range in price from $65 to $110.

JANIE COMITO

❦

Janie Bear

Janie Comito's bears have been constantly evolving since 1981.

"I get daily ideas for new bears," she says, "and love costuming each one by whim from an ever-changing collection of antique fabrics, lace pieces, and trims."

Miniatures are her favorites; she enjoys the challenge of working small, and one-of-a-kind bears are her specialty. They range in size from 1 3/4 to 10 inches high.

Her editions are perhaps two or four bears because she often works with difficult-to-find materials.

"What distinguishes my bears," she says, "is the gentle influence of times past. People comment on the sweetness of expression of my creations; I'm known for Victorian costuming from vintage fabrics."

"Janie Bears" are available from their creator or from The Owl and the Pussycat in Ft. Myers, Florida.

Value: They range in price from $85 to $200.

"Nicholas and Poley" by Janie Comito, 1987. "Nicholas," a 6-inch bear with wire armatured body, wears a Father Christmas robe and hat and drives a wooden sleigh pulled by "Poley," the 9-inch-long mohair polar bear. *Photo by Carol-Lynn Rössel Waugh.*

BARBARA CONLEY

❀❀❀

Roley Bear Company

For Barbara Conley, making teddy bears is a part-time project. Full-time, she is a professional landscape artist. Her paintings of rural America evoke nostalgia, revealing the Californian's interest in antiques and historic preservation. They have won many awards, including a silver medal from Grumbacher.

Antiques and nostalgia led Barbara to bears, and she had quite a collection before she began making originals in 1983. She wanted to make just one bear, a modern interpretation of what she was looking for in old ones.

"I tried to get the look of the Margaret Strong Steiff bears in my work, with some success, but not quite," she says.

"Jeremy" by Barbara Conley is 20 inches tall and made of off-white mohair. He is fully jointed and has German glass eyes, brown embroidered nose and mouth, and a growler voice box. *Photo courtesy of Barbara Conley.*

"Sandy" by Barbara Conley is 24 inches tall, fully jointed, and made of honey mohair with excelsior stuffing. He has antique shoe button eyes and a growler and is wearing an antique collar. The painting behind him is the first in a limited edition. It depicts him and two other bears and is by Barbara Conley. *Photo courtesy of Barbara Conley.*

Barbara achieved an endearing mixture of nostalgic appeal and an artist's sensitivity, most evident in her appealing faces.

"I like happy bears," she says, "with an innocent, honest look and just a slight lift to one side of the mouth."

Almost all of her teddies, ranging in size from $2^7/_8$ to 28 inches, are mohair (some are from old coats), with glass eyes. The biggest are excelsior-stuffed. All are fully jointed and some even have yes/no or no/no mechanisms. Only about 5% are dressed.

But there aren't a lot of them. Teddy experiments fit into cracks in studio schedules.

"I can go weeks without making a bear," Barbara says, "then reverse where that is all I do. Painting is full-time for me."

Because of limited production (about 75 to 100 annually), she and her daughter, Tracy Roe—who shares the Roley Bear Company logo, each producing her own bears—sell primarily at shows, or through "Bears in the Woods" in Los Gatos, California.

Barbara's editions are limited by boredom. "As in my painting, I dislike repeating something just because it might sell," she says. "There are so many styles and ways to make a bear. One of these days I will make that one special bear, and then I may move on to the next challenge."

Value: "Roley Bears" range in price from $95 to $650.

NANCY CROWE

❧

Pearls

Nancy Crowe of Lansing, Michigan, began a small craft business in 1982 as a means of staying home with young children. In 1985 she designed her first original rabbit pattern under the name of "Pearls." In 1987 she began working in mohair and expanded her designs to include bears.

She specializes in dressed character bears, the ideas for many of which come from a year spent living in England. Among them is "Molly Malone," 12 inches tall, pushing her cart of cockles and mussels.

The idea for perhaps her finest bear, however, comes from her own midwestern heritage. "Ma-wa-qua" (Little Bear) is dressed in a costume found in the 1850s with Indians involved in the Great Lakes fur trade. His hand-beaded leather coat, made with the help of Rose M. De Land, an Ottawa and Chippewa Indian of the Burt Lake Band, is modeled after

"Molly Malone" by Nancy Crowe is a 12-inch-tall ginger mohair bear dressed in a costume typical of Ireland in the 1850s. She pushes her handmade cart of cockles and mussels. *Photo by Kim Kauffman.*

those made following European designs but with Native American materials.

Crowe bears are generally 11 to 16 inches tall, made from imported mohair, and are fully jointed, with glass eyes. They are made in signed, limited editions and are available directly from the artist.

Value: They range in price from $130 to $250.

SUZANNE DE PEE

❀❀❀

Honeypot Bears™

From a hobby started in 1983, Suzanne De Pee's bearmaking has blossomed into a full-time business. Some of her designs have a lovely old-

"Geraldine" by Suzanne De Pee is 22 inches tall and made of soft German synthetic fur that resembles angora. She has brown glass eyes and pigskin pads and is filled with polyester. Her homespun plaid bow is cream and rose. *Photo by Suzanne De Pee.*

fashioned look and sport a distinctive innocent expression. She is well known for her mischievous tricycle-riding teddies.

Chiefly made of mohair, "Honeypot Bears"℠ are fully jointed and see the world through glass eyes. Most are undressed. They range in size from 8 to 26 inches tall.

Suzanne has cut back to producing perhaps 100 bears a year. Her editions are never more than 200 to 300 of any teddy.

Today much of Suzanne's time is spent representing the work of other bearmakers, selling bears at shows, and attending to her mail-order bear business. (A catalog is available for $3.) New designs must fit into this busy schedule. "Basically," she says, "I sell mail order."

Value: Honeypot Bears℠ *range in price from $75 to $260.*

BRENDA DEWEY

❧❧

Soda Fountain Bears

Brenda Dewey is perhaps best known for her fantasy bears: silk-garbed fairies, elves, wizards, and even a "Guardian of the Fairy Folk" toting a wounded gnome bear and a wee fairy bear. Her sense of whimsy is irrepressible, whether her teddies are 6 or 36 inches tall.

"B.J. and the Rescue" (© 1989 Brenda Dewey) is 12 inches tall, is made of mohair, and has glass eyes. "B.J." has just rescued a mouse from the trap but looks as if he has trouble removing his hand from it. *Photo courtesy of Brenda Dewey.*

Fully jointed and made of mohair, alpaca, imported acrylic, or rayon, they have glass eyes and are almost always dressed or accessorized.

The Clinton, New York, resident began making bears in 1976, when her second son, Brian, was born prematurely. She began selling them on the crafts circuit in 1980 but really entered the "bear business" in 1985. The name "Soda Fountain Bears" dates from that year, when Brenda's bears were made with heads of fifteen different flavors, and customers could order a single, double, or triple scoop bear ice cream cone.

Today's "Soda Fountain Bears" can be almost serious and traditional, with a Victorian flavor. Her best-known creation is "Humble Bumble," a hiker bear whose friend, "Jumble" the mouse, rides in his backpack.

Except for a little help from her family with cutting out, Brenda does all of her own designing and bearmaking, and she delights in one-of-a-kind projects. Editions range from 25 to 50 bears and are often limited by boredom.

"I am usually easy to spot at a show," she says. "Just look for a beanie hat!" She attends from six to nine shows annually, wholesales to twenty shops, and sells by direct mail.

Value: "Soda Fountain Bears" range in price from $75 to $500.

HOLLY DYER

❦

Hollybearys

"Pete" by Holly Dyer is stuffed with plastic beans. He is 18 inches of fully jointed, flexible floppiness. He comes in mohair with glass eyes or acrylic with safety eyes. *Photo by Roberta L. Hogan.*

Holly Cramer Dyer grew up with a collection of dolls and bears, so it's no wonder she turned to bearmaking. She started out using purchased bear patterns, but they were inadequate. So Holly and her mother collaborated on a design, called "Watersmith" after their street, and "Hollybearys" were born.

Holly's bears today are made of synthetics or mohair, and their pieces reflect the fabric used. Stuffed with polyester fiberfill or plastic beans, they have glass or acrylic eyes and are fully jointed. Most have decided humps and are pigeon-toed. Their printed foot tags make them easily recognizable.

Holly and her mother make about 200 bears a year. They range in size from 3 1/4 to 18 inches.

She sells primarily by mail but occasionally sells at shows and to selected shops.

Value: "Hollybearys" range in price from $45 to $150.

PATRICIA S. FICI

Trishka's Treasures

Pat Fici's first plush animal was a guinea pig, designed in response to her children's pleas to adopt a sibling of their preschool class pet. From there she branched out into stegosauruses, unicorns, and, in 1985, teddy bears.

"I use only my own designs for the bears and their costumes," she says. "I do work entirely alone, which consequently limits my annual production while allowing it to be classified as 100% artist-made. All of my bears are effectively members of limited editions, and although the size of the edition may not be specified, each bear is numbered as he/she is completed. (The largest official edition size I might currently consider would be fifty pieces.)"

Pat's bears have won prizes, including Golden Teddy awards in 1988 and 1989, and have grown from toy to collector status. Made from

"The Seamstress" by Pat Fici won a Golden Teddy award in 1988. She is 17 inches tall and made of gold mohair, with glass eyes, a voice box, and leather pads. Her unique knee joint design permits her to stand or sit. Clothed in bloomers, slip, and a navy calico dress with lace trims, she holds a piece of old quilting. Edition of 50. *Photo courtesy of Pat Fici.*

"Oh What a Face!" by Pat Fici is fully jointed, made of mohair, and approximately 15 inches tall. Her eyes are glass. She is dressed in a pinafore/apron and gazes into a mirror. *Photo courtesy of Pat Fici.*

imported plush or mohair, they are fully jointed, usually have glass eyes, and boast innovations such as the jointed knees on "The Seamstress."

"As my work has progressed and matured," she says, "I more and more frequently envision my bears as sculptures, albeit with somewhat fluid natures given their ability to change poses. This is especially true with the 'My Lady' series of bears, including 'But Woman's Work Is Never Done,' 'Oh, What a Face!,' and 'The Seamstress,' along with my most recent bear, 'St. Francis.' Costuming and accessorizing have become an integral part of the final persona of these bears, as with most of my work."

"Trishka's Treasures" are available directly from Pat Fici.

Value: They range in price from $50 to $450.

SUE ELLEN FOSKEY

❦

The Nostalgic Bear Company

Sue Ellen Foskey began designing bears as a hobby in 1983. Selling first at craft shows, she perfected designs as bears found homes. In 1985 she produced her first effort in mohair, a 12-inch-tall, fully jointed teddy called "Nostalgic Bear." The edition of 100 sold by 1986.

"Frank Beardue" by Sue Foskey is 9 inches tall and fully jointed. Made of mohair with glass eyes, he was designed for the Delmarva Chicken Festival in 1989. Only 20 bears were in his edition; one was presented to Frank Perdue of chicken fame. *Photo courtesy of Sue Foskey.*

When demand for her work exceeded her ability to fill orders, the Delaware bearmaker formed, with her husband, Randall, a cottage industry company employing five to ten seamstresses and craftpersons to assist in manufacturing her designs. These women do piecework in their homes, each with a particular bearmaking job. This gives the bears consistency.

Sue now does the designing and the faces; in 1989 the company produced around 1,200 bears. Editions are limited to 100 bears but may be smaller.

"We named our firm The Nostalgic Bear Company because Sue's favorite bears are those she calls her 'Antique Reproductions,' " her husband explains. These bears are "distressed" with a secret process, are stuffed with straw, and have old shoe button eyes. *

Ranging in size from 6 1/2 to 28 inches, most Foskey bears are fully jointed, have glass eyes, and are made of all-new materials, including imported mohair. Styles range from reproductions to contemporary "art teddies," including a bear astride an elephant. About 25% of the line is partially attired with a hat or a collar or a simple vest or coat.

"I generally like to see a bear underdressed rather than overdressed," Sue says, "because I am more intrigued with the design of the bear itself."

"Nostalgic Bear Company" bears are sold through many fine teddy bear shops as well as directly at shows or by mail order.

Value: They range in price from $45 to $400.

*See Antique Bear section for Sue Foskey's restoration work.

GLORIA J. FRANKS

☙

By Goose Creek

Gloria Franks moved into the teddy bear world from the doll world after she and her husband moved to their farm in West Virginia. She had been making a variety of cloth dolls and displaying them at doll and bear shows. Here she made contact with antique bears, fell in love with them, and made the decision to make teddies.

Antique styling began influencing her work, but in 1983 she started

"Appalachia" by Gloria Franks is 20 inches tall. She is fully jointed and made of golden tan mohair with glass eyes and is stuffed with polyester fiberfill. She is dressed in a muslin pinafore and panties with ecru country lace trim. On her head is a baby's-breath wreath. *Photo courtesy of Gloria Franks.*

developing her own look, combining the best of the old with a contemporary flair, always looking back to her dollmaking days for techniques and inspiration.

Today "By Goose Creek" designs (named after the waterway on the Franks's farm) are easily identifiable as Gloria's (and her husband Mike's) work by their innocent, inquiring expressions.

"We make two or three dressed bears a year, and these are my favorites," Gloria says. "Mike likes them more traditional." The Franks have ten or eleven bears in their line each year, adding four to five and retiring others. Limited editions usually run to 150; total annual production is approximately 600.

The fully jointed, glass-eyed bears range in size from 8 to 26 inches and are made of mohair by Mike and Gloria. Family members do much of the sewing and knitting for them, from Gloria's designs.

Value: "By Goose Creek" bears range in price from $66 to $240.

THE REV. CHESTER D. FREEMAN, JR.

Baskets and Bears

"The Freeman Backpacker Bear" (logo and trademark of the classic Freeman Bears, © 1983 Chester Freeman) is 13 inches tall. He is made of pure silver gray German mohair and has antique black shoe button eyes, embroidered nose and mouth, and pure wool felt pads. He wears a handmade black ash splint Adirondack basket with red and green straps. *Photo by Dale Duchesne.*

Chester Freeman began making bears in 1982 during his chaplaincy at the University of Massachusetts in Amherst in response to a challenge from a friend. He found such acceptance for his work, both as a solacing object in hospital ministry and as a commercial product, that he went into the bear business full-time in 1985.

Chester's bears are classic in style, using a pattern he designed and refined until he felt it matched his idea of the "perfect teddy bear." Perhaps his best-known teddy wears a handmade basket backpack made by his partner, John Maguire, the other half of "Baskets and Bears."

They come in three sizes—10, 13, and 16 inches—are fully jointed, and are made from specially dyed imported mohair. Half are dressed, a new development for the upstate New Yorker. He hand-produces from 250 to 300 a year. Special editions, when done, are limited to 100 or 150. He also produces charming teddy bear muffs.

Chester, whose work in two sizes has been produced commercially by Merrythought Ltd. in England, sees making bears as a logical outgrowth of his ministry:

"I design and make bears as a symbol of love," he says, "a love that is patient and kind, always ready to excuse, to trust, to hope, and to endure."

Freeman bears are available at selected shops or by mail order.

Value: They range in price from $98 to $145.

ELAINE FUJITA-GAMBLE

Fujita-Gamble Teddies

Elaine Gamble began collecting bears in 1973 when a friend brought a stuffed bear to her from Yellowstone National Park. Then Beverly Port introduced her to antiques, and she never has looked back.

Collecting led to bearmaking. "I played with several teddy bear patterns while I worked during the summer for the park department," she says. "I used simple patterns to teach the children how to sew. I didn't start designing my own bears to sell until late in 1979."

Fashioned along the lines of the German Hermann bears, her first original was 5 inches tall, a size she still prefers, although Fujita-Gamble teddies at times reach 15 inches.

A full-time physical education teacher who loves playing in sports leagues, Elaine squeezes bearmaking into corners of her busy schedule,

"Theodora" by Elaine Fujita-Gamble is 2 inches tall. Fully jointed, she is made of synthetic pile stuffed with cotton and is dressed in trims with old rhinestones, pearls, and beads. *Photo by George Comito.*

preferring working on new projects and one-of-a-kind teddies to filling orders.

Her work is distinguished by meticulous attention to details and fine craftsmanship. Knowledge of antiques gives her a visual vocabulary to draw on when creating modern interpretations of anything from traditional teddies to "locket bears," which open to reveal hidden surprises.

Editions are very small; Elaine does all of the work and limits herself to the small number of orders she can fill and the preferred experiments and innovations she brings to shows.

Value: Fujita-Gamble bears range in price from $75 to $100.

DIANE GARD

✿✿✿

A Bear With a Heart

Diane Gard began her business, "A Bear With a Heart," in 1983 after experiments in bearmaking turned into an avocation. Early Gard bears were patterned after antiques and made from vintage materials, but they already had a distinctive style: long slender limbs, a traditional humped back, and a wedge-shaped head with quizzical expression.

Made of mohair, with glass eyes, and ranging from 16 to 26 inches tall, every one of Diane's bears has a heart affixed to its chest.

In 1988 she began making attenuated fashion bears, many of them collaborative efforts. In 1989 she started a line of similarly designed fairy tale characters.

Diane is very prolific; her bears are available not only directly from her but in shops throughout the United States.

Value: They range in price from $125 to $450.

"Elizabeth" by Diane Gard is 15 inches tall and made of amber rose antique flower-patterned mohair. At her neck is a piece of antique tatting.

DOLORES GROSSECK

❧

Bears of Southampton

Whenever one of Dolores Grosseck's bears says what she wants it to say artistically, she credits the design education she received at Drexel University in Philadelphia.

"The department stressed stretching ideas and integrating heretofore unrelated objects into a project and make them relate," she says. "As a result I try to mix media, such as putting clay noses on bears."

She began making her large (20 to 24 inches tall) bears in 1986, using them as a vehicle for design concepts.

Dolores Grosseck's 22-inch-tall, fully jointed mohair lady holds a nest of birds in her overskirt apron. *Photo by Richard Heggs.*

Dolores Grosseck's 24-inch-tall mohair bear with felt paw pads is fully jointed and wears a fur-trimmed winter coat, a feather-trimmed picture bonnet, and lots of jewelry (© 1989). *Photo by Richard Heggs.*

"I've kept the body somewhat traditional," she says, "and choose to rely on the basic form relating to other media. There are many ways to reinterpret an art form, to reillustrate it. I use environmental props and relate them to my bear. A hat, bird, button, etc., will provide the springboard."

Often Dolores's bears wear clothing reminiscent of gentler times. Their props seem to come from already-established personalities.

"I feel I do bears that come with a script," she says. "They're playing a role already, almost as if they had a life before the customers buy them. It is up to the customer to continue the play."

The Pennsylvania designer completes fewer than 100 bears a year and offers them for sale at shows or selected shops. Most are one of a kind or in "editions" of two or three.

Value: "Bears of Southampton" range in price from $250 to $300.

MARY HAGGARD

❧

Haggard Huggables

"Chauncey" (© 1988 Mary Haggard) is 9 inches tall and made of cinnamon-hued synthetic fur. He is fully jointed, with black glass eyes and a hand-shaped black vinyl nose. His paws are black suede cloth, and he wears a white collar with a blue and green plaid bow and eyeglasses. Made in a signed, numbered edition limited to 50 bears. *Photo by Mary Haggard.*

Mary Haggard is an equine and wildlife artist with an international reputation. She has worked in at least three countries and has been featured in approximately a dozen equine magazines.

In 1986 she designed her first teddy bear, a large, unjointed cubby, a bit more realistic than most bears. Now she makes fully jointed bears ranging in size from 7 to 23 inches tall.

Generally made of synthetic fur, with shoe button or glass eyes and often hand-shaped vinyl noses, Haggard bears are remarkably detailed, featuring carefully shaded muzzles and, in the case of "Hubert" and his little brother "Huey," the white "collar" common to black bears, as well as a tan muzzle and eye spots.

Her large unjointed pandas look so real, hugging them is the next best thing to holding a real baby panda. They have unique paw pads carefully sewn on by hand, shiny black eyes that almost water, and vinyl eyelids and nose. Each has his own Chinese name, written on his paw in both English and Chinese.

All of Mary's bears have endearing expressions and are three-dimensional testimony to her abiding interest in wildlife, managing to look "real" while at the same time retaining a "teddy bear" quality.

"Haggard Huggables" are made in limited editions and are signed and dated.

Value: They range in price from $65 to $175.

BILLEE HENDERSON

❧

Billee's Beasties

"Honey Bun" by Billee Henderson is 19 1/2 inches tall, fully jointed, and made of wavy mohair, with glass eyes and growler. *Photo by Carol-Lynn Rössel Waugh.*

The gentle expressions of Billee Henderson's bears say a lot about the personality of their creator.

A textile and clothing major at the University of Maryland, Billee put her training to practical use for thirty years, designing and sewing clothing for herself and five children.

Her offspring finally grown, in 1982 she sewed her first teddy bears, selling them at neighborhood craft shows. They developed into classic fully jointed mohair originals with heart-tugging expressions, in sizes from 7 to 33 inches.

Often Billee's best-sellers derive from special requests, such as 33-inch-tall "Alexander the Great," who won a first prize in 1989 at a teddy bear convention.

"I do a bear at a time and then go on to something else," Billee says. "And my bears seem to be getting bigger and bigger. I do all my designing and production myself; I can't make more than about 120 a year."

Billee attends four teddy bear conventions a year, both to sell work and to commune with other artists. Her work is also available by mail order or from shops.

Value: "Billee's Beasties" range in price from $60 to $395.

DEE HOCKENBERRY

❧

Bears N Things

Dee Hockenberry began making bears in 1982. They range in size from 10 to 18 inches tall.

Hockenberry bears have a wistful look and traditional conformation. Dee is perhaps best known for her elaborate jesters. Approximately 75% of her bears are clothed; sometimes permanently, often elegantly, with good color sense.

"Father Christmas" by Dee Hockenberry is 18 inches tall and made of champagne mohair with glass eyes. He wears a burgundy velvet robe with fur trim and gold cord, his leaf crown adorned with silk holly. He holds a staff with green bells on it. *Photo courtesy of Dee Hockenberry.*

"I like dressed bears," she says, "because it is exciting to stretch the imagination when an idea unfolds."

Dee does most of the construction work herself. Her husband makes the bears' joints. She sometimes has help with clothing.

She produces 300 to 500 bears annually. Editions range from one-of-a-kinds to her large jesters, of which only five to ten of each are made, to editions of fifty bears for catalogs. All others are unlimited.

Hockenberry bears are available at teddy shops, by direct mail, and at one or two shows per year.

Value: They range in price from $70 to $500.

DONNA HODGES

The Bearons of La Jolla

Lifelong San Diego, California, resident Donna Hodges often names the teddy bears she has made since about 1983 after family members, especially her nine grandchildren.

These often elaborately garbed fully jointed teddies range in size from 5½ to 24 inches.

Donna excels in "packaging concepts." Her teddies come in trunks or fancily trimmed bandboxes, or they may have an armoire full of clothes. The charming period clothing she designs for approximately half her bears

"Sophia" by Donna Hodges is 7 inches tall and made of white llama with black glass eyes and Ultrasuède paws. She wears an old-fashioned pink silk dress and pantaloons trimmed with silk ribbons and roses. She lives in a custom pink hatbox decorated with dried flower arrangements. A limited edition of 50. *Photo by James A. Hodges.*

is rife with meticulous detailing and special touches. In many ways, Donna's teddy bears are furry dolls.

Her almost-undressed bears show off their mohair or llama fur and glass eyes with perhaps just a scarf or an accessory.

Donna designs the bears and costumes. They are then cut and sewn by an excellent seamstress. Their joints are riveted by a pneumatic riveter. Their fiberfill is stuffed by machine. Donna does the faces of all of the bears. "The people who help me are selected for their expertise in the sewing field," Donna says. "They are creative and often assist me by offering valuable suggestions."

In 1989 the "Bearons of La Jolla" produced around 600 teddies.

Donna now sells exclusively wholesale. Made in editions of usually 100 or less, her bears can be found in shops throughout the United States, Canada, and Japan.

Value: They range in price from $100 to $860.

MARY HOLSTAD

Mary Holstad's Collectibles

"Amanda and Friend" (© 1989 Mary Holstad). Made of mohair, "Amanda" is 15 inches tall and fully jointed. She has glass eyes and wears a wine-colored dress. Her cream-colored kitty is made of synthetic plush. *Photo by Carol-Lynn Rössel Waugh*.

Mary Holstad has always loved art. In high school she won the junior and senior art awards. In 1983 she studied drafting, technical illustrating, and computer-aided drafting. By the time she graduated she was already hooked on making bears. In 1984 she introduced "Katie's New Kitten," her first teddy bear with a pet.

Pets—especially kittens—set Mary's bears apart. The left arms on some of her mohair bears are specially shaped to hold a kitten with an awkward childish gesture. When kitty is removed, the arm can be raised to the bear's eyes in a fretful, pouting pose.

Her unjointed teddies are silky soft and wonderful to hug or cry into, and they share the same innocent expressions of her jointed bears, highlighted by painstaking clipping done with a small scissors. Her teddies have won two Golden Teddy awards.

Mary works full-time making bears and finishes about 300 a year. In her spare time she does detailed pastel drawings.

"Each bear has to have that tug at the heart to please me," she says. "Making bears is very rewarding. Each bear is like a child being born."

Value: Mary Holstad Collectibles range in price from $85 to $475. Special orders are higher.

"Mandy" (© 1987 Mary Holstad) is a floppy 15-inch bear made of buttery-soft synthetic plush. She wears a pink hand-knit sweater. *Photo by Carol-Lynn Rössel Waugh.*

HILLARY HULEN

❧

Heidibears and Heidihares

Hillary Hulen is a naturalist by training and inclination. A former ranger for the National Park Service, she has worked as a biological illustrator for scientific journals and studied art at the Smithsonian Institution.

Bearmaking entered her life in 1980, when she sought a profession in tune with her rural lifestyle. Her first original bears financed a birdwatching trip in Mexico and gave her an alternative to city commuting, so she decided to become a full-time bearmaker in 1982.

Hillary's bears, most of which are undressed, as befits a naturalist's teddies, range in size from 3 to 36 inches and are made only of 100%

This off-white bear by Hillary Hulen is fully jointed. He has glass eyes and brown embroidered nose, mouth, and claws, and he wears a heart-shaped potpourri around his neck on a ribbon. *Photo courtesy of Hillary Hulen.*

mohair or alpaca. She designs at least a couple of new bears a month, working long hours with her husband, David Ruegg, who joints them and supervises construction. "Without David and his support," Hillary says, "I could not produce as many bears as I do." Together, they turn out 500 to 1,000 bears and hares annually. Editions are limited to 50.

Heidihares, as Hillary calls her rabbits, were inspired by her gray rabbit, McBuggs, and have become perhaps more identified with the couple than the bears. Both benefit from her knowledge of wildlife and her ability to re-create it in three dimensions, with just a touch of fantasy—a basket of berries or a jaunty bonnet—thrown in for appeal. All are produced with meticulous detailing and craftsmanship.

"Heidihares and Heidibears" are available by direct mail, from "The Owl and the Pussycat" in Florida, and "Kits and Kaboodle" in Indiana.

Value: They range in price from $75 to $575.

MAGGIE IACONO

❦

Maggie Made

Maggie Iacono learned to sew at an early age. Her bearmaking was a natural progression from cloth dollmaking, which she began in 1981. As her skill in dollmaking progressed, so did her bearmaking. One became a release for the other.

"Dorothy and Gregory" by Maggie Iacono are 11 inches tall, made of mohair, and stuffed with fiberfill. Dorothy's dress is blue gingham with a white blouse. She has white lace-trimmed socks and red rollerskates. Gregory has a blue pin-striped shirt and denim pants. Around his neck is a fisherman's sweater. He is also wearing blue roller skates. *Photo by Maggie Iacono.*

Although her bears do grow as tall as 10 inches (a few even taller), Maggie is best known for her 3-inch-tall dressed mohair teddies.

"All my bears are dressed," she says. "Sometimes I hate covering up their beautiful fur, but when I look at them they just seem 'bare' without clothes. I can do more humorous things with their clothing that I wouldn't do with a doll, so it is a different creative outlet."

Maggie's annual output varies from 70 to 140 bears, and her editions are limited by personal preference. They can be purchased directly or from a few select shops.

Value: "Maggie Made" bears range in price from $50 to $250.

CHARLOTTE JOYNT

Sabema

"Haggerty" by Charlotte Joynt is made of mohair, is fully jointed, and has a sculpted leather nose and glass eyes. He wears Irish tweeds and carries on his back a basket filled with real Irish peat. *Photo courtesy of Charlotte Joynt.*

Charlotte Joynt named her bearmaking business "Sabema" after her three daughters; Sarah, Beth, and Maggie.

She has been making bears since the fall of 1982, working first with tweeds and synthetics, progressing to mohair and alpaca as she developed her own patterns and style.

These expressive-faced fully jointed teddies range in size from 7 1/2 to 24 inches in height, have glass eyes and sometimes sculpted-leather noses. Very few are dressed.

An exception is "Haggerty," a limited-edition Irish bear dressed in

"Benjamin" by Charlotte Joynt is made of imported mohair. He is fully jointed and has a sculpted leather nose. *Photo courtesy of Charlotte Joynt.*

tweeds and carrying a backpack basket full of real Irish peat. Most of Charlotte's bears are "boys."

Because her family is young, bearmaking is part-time for the Iowa resident, and annual production is small. Editions are limited to 25. They are available by direct mail or at select shops.

Value: "Sabema" bears range in price from $60 to $300.

DEBBIE KESLING

Granny's Locket Bears

Since making her first bear in 1982, Debbie Kesling's teddies have undergone many evolutionary changes. Ranging upward in size from $3/4$ inch, they are fully jointed. Her "standard size" bears are made from mohair or alpaca and have antique shoe button eyes; tiny teddies are fashioned from

"Alice" by Debbie Kesling is fully jointed, 13 inches tall, and made of mohair with antique shoe button eyes and Ultrasuède pads. She is stuffed with polyester fiberfill and wears an antique lace collar. *Photo by John Kesling.*

"Bellhop" by Debbie Kesling is 2 inches tall, fully jointed, and made of upholstery fabric. He has enameled eyes, 14k-gold buttons, and Ultrasuède pads. He is stuffed with cotton batting. The costume is a permanent part of the bear. *Photo by Carol-Lynn Rössel Waugh.*

special low-nap flexible upholstery fabric and have special eyes Debbie developed.

Debbie loves making her bears, and it shows. She spends hours developing new patterns and personalities, searching for accessories and matching them with fabrics to enhance each bear's character. She stitches into each bear's face a sweet imploring innocence. But she rarely dresses them, except when the "fur" costume is part of the body.

"I'm not a dressmaker," she said when asked about costuming. "I'm involved in birthing bears, not making their wardrobes."

In 1988 Debbie left her job as a corporate personnel manager to devote all of her time to bearmaking. She sells her bears directly: by mail or at shows, and rarely accepts wholesale accounts.

Value: "Granny's Locket" bears range in price from $120 to $220.

JACQUE KUDNER

❧

Jacquebears

"Timely" by Jacque Kudner is a 20-inch mohair bear wearing an antique pocket watch in a built-in pocket. He is her best seller, also offered in a 15-inch-tall version. *Photo courtesy of Jacque Kudner.*

Jacque Kudner has had a longtime love affair with fiber art. She began sewing as a teenager and soon began making her own clothes. At the University of Utah she earned a degree in fine art with emphasis on textiles and education. When she graduated, she taught high school art for five years while working on a master's degree in fibers.

In 1985, while she was working as an interior designer, she began making bears in an attempt to add the perfect bear to her newborn son's collection, and as a creative outlet because she was newly housebound with an infant.

She likes her fully jointed, glass-eyed mohair bears to resemble antiques but constantly changes them in an attempt to get what she terms "the perfect expression." Current designs feature curved arms and legs, a wide forehead, and big feet, as well as increasingly detailed costuming.

Her favorite bears wear antique treasures or are characters from old

"Santa" by Jacque Kudner is 15 inches tall and made of mohair. He wears a mink-trimmed off-white wool coat with a leather satchel-belt; a hand-woven basket rests on his back. His arms are full of antique toys. He is limited to 25 pieces. *Photo courtesy of Jacque Kudner.*

books. In 1989 she offered five different Santa Bears, to meet the demands of "Christmas collectors."

Jacque averages 200 limited-edition bears a year, and her prices change with improvements and costuming.

Value: Early "Jacquebears" cost $40. Today the most expensive costs approximately $500.

BEV MILLER LANDSTRA

Bev Landstra Collectables

"Shirley Teddy" by Bev Landstra is 9½ inches tall, made of synthetic fur, and fully jointed. Her dress is white with red dots and a lace neck ruffle. *Photo by Roger Holm.*

Beverly Miller Landstra has been making things since she was little. In school she always took at least one art or sewing class, making her own patterns, and had the best-dressed dolls in town.

As she grew up, she turned hobby into profession, working as a tailor in a men's shop, sewing suits and tuxedos; but in 1981, when her son turned three, Bev decided to resume early penchants and whipped up a teddy bear for him. One bear led to more, and, turning full circle, hobby became profession.

Landstra bears stand $1\frac{1}{2}$ to 14 inches tall, are made of mohair or synthetics, and are fully jointed; 75% are elaborately dressed.

Most of their noses are made from "Marble-X," which is modeled and dried. This is the last thing done.

Early bears included occupational bears, bears named with puns for famous people, and her famous "Pregnant Bear" (the latter the result of a happy accident—the first "Pregnant Bear" was put together backwards).

Bev does other soft sculpture: dogs, rabbits, kittens, unicorns, and horses—portraits of real animals. But bears allow her whimsy to come through. She is perhaps best known for "Shirley Teddy" and for bears that look like their owners.

Special editions number 50 bears. Bev makes about 300 a year with just a little help from her mother, who knits sweaters or scarves; they can be found in bear shops.

Value: "Bev Landstra Collectables" range in price from $40 to $500.

TAMMIE LAWRENCE

Tammie's Teddies

"Papa and Baby Tab" by Tammie Lawrence are 16 and 7 inches tall, respectively. Both one-of-a-kind bears are made of distressed mohair, partially stuffed with cotton and with excelsior. Their pads are "worn through" to reveal the excelsior. They have glass eyes. The baby is dressed in an antique doll's dress. *Photo courtesy of Tammie Lawrence.*

Mohair scraggly and worn, paw pads patched, aged shoe button eyes shining and wise, Tammie Lawrence's teddies slump eloquently with the posture of bears reshaped by years of fervent caresses.

Though they look, feel, and even smell the part, these teddies are far from antiques. Fond reflections of teddy bears that might have been, they're the product of a designer who uses the past as a common visual and emotional language, conjuring up imaginary playmates her customers wish they'd had.

Tammie began making bears in 1982 with the intent of duplicating an antique bear in a photograph. She sold her first efforts, dressed to speci-fication, to a friend who owned an antiques store. They sold so well she launched into a full-time bearmaking career, working seven days a week producing her own designs, striving to make "the one perfect bear."

Made of mohair treated with a secret process to look old, they range from tots to oldsters; and their clothing, either antique or made from nat-ural fibers, accentuates their definite personalities. Original designs ranging in height from 5 to 25 inches, they bring to mind bears of the first three

"Tiny Theodora" by Tammie Lawrence is 10 inches tall, a one-of-a-kind bear made of very distressed mohair. She has glass eyes, and her felt pads are "worn through," revealing excelsior inside. She is dressed in antique doll clothing. *Photo courtesy of Tammie Lawrence.*

"Benjamin Bear" by Tammie Lawrence is 17 inches tall and made of distressed mohair. He is a 1920s-style bear with long arms and small feet and is one-of-a-kind. *Photo courtesy of Tammie Lawrence.*

decades of this century. Never copies, these teddies are loving recreations of imaginary memories.

Tammie keeps fresh and challenged by switching styles every three months or so. She makes about thirty bears a month; her editions run to 25 (50 in large ones), and all the bears are her own work. Much of the dressing is now done by an expert seamstress to her designs.

Many of her bears are one of a kind. "I never enjoy staying with one edition very long," she says. "I feel penned in and don't feel I am being creative and artistic, and I start searching for a new project."

"Tammie's Teddies" are available through select shops and only occasionally, by special request, from their designer.

Value: They range in price from $75 to $875.

ALTHEA LEISTIKOW

❦

Bears by Althea

Althea Leistikow began designing and making teddies in 1984. She is best known for classic-looking bears with appealing faces, clean finishing work, clean lines, and use of vintage fabrics.

Presently about 20% of her bears, which range in size from 6 to 27 inches, are dressed, some with vintage hats and collars, others in fashions with an old-time look. "Personally," she says, "the bear under the clothes is more important to me than the clothes."

Althea makes 300 bears a year and does all her own work. Some editions are only 10 bears, but they can reach 100 at times. Each bear has a handmade tag on the back above the left leg.

She has won prizes for her work, including the Golden Teddy award in 1987.

Althea sells at conventions and shows and by mail order.

Value: "Bears by Althea" range in price from $72 to $650.

"Teddy Goldenwood" by Althea Leistikow is 16 inches tall, fully jointed, and made of mohair. *Photo courtesy of Althea Leistikow.*

WENDY LOCKWOOD

Country and Bears

"Golden Griz," 15 inches tall, by Wendy Lockwood, is made of hand-dyed gold-peach grizzled alpaca. He is fully jointed and has black glass eyes. *Photo courtesy of Wendy Lockwood.*

When Wendy Lockwood made her first bear in 1984, she drew on her studies in clothing and textiles and her background in fashion merchandising to propel it into "Country and Bears" in the fall of that year.

Wendy's well-constructed teddies have a classic look and endearing faces. "My bears get a lot of their personality from their faces," she says. "I have been told by many customers that they 'talk' to them across a room."

Most Lockwood bears are made from alpaca, mohair, or imported plush and range in size from 6 to 23 inches. About 25%, as of fall 1989, are dressed. "I think there must be a reason for the clothes," Wendy says. "Too many people cover a bad bear with great clothes."

Wendy does all of the construction, designing, and sewing; her husband, Kip, cuts and tightens joints and stuffs for her. "I really feel it's important for an artist to do all of the work himself," she says. "Too many artists are turning into factories with lots of hired help. These aren't really their bears anymore."

About 500 Lockwood bears are "born" every year. Regular editions run from 60 to 200; special editions run from 10 to 50. They are signed and numbered on a sewn-in tag on the right leg.

Wendy's bears are available at shows, by mail or phone orders, and from shops.

Value: "Country and Bears" teddies range in price from $62 to $300.

LYNN LUMLEY

❧❧

Grandma Lynn's Teddybears

"Grandma" Lynn Lumley's little teddy bears are handfuls of personality, handcrafted from imported llama and other fine fabrics.

These 4½- to 6½-inch, fully jointed teddies are easily spotted by their endearing, imploring expressions.

A fully jointed 5½-inch-tall little girl bear by Lynn Lumley. She is made of alpaca, wears a ribbon-trimmed Ultrasuède bonnet, and offers her fully jointed porcelain doll for inspection. *Photo by Carol-Lynn Rössel Waugh.*

"I spend hours, sometimes, on a face," Lynn says. "I try to make a face that seems alive to me. If it's not just right, I change and rechange whatever I have to as many times as I have to until I can see and feel he is real."

All of Lynn's teddies have a signature embroidery on one footpad, and she extensively employs "fancy work" stitchery to embellish their hats, bonnets, and jackets, which are often fashioned from ultrasuede and adorned with ribbons, lace, and flower rosettes. Some wear clothes from calicoes and eyelet. Others she gives a porcelain doll or frog companion. Lynn does all of the dressing herself.

Working in her little Carson City, Nevada, apartment, she completes 250 or 350 teddies a year, all of them signed and numbered limited editions. "I'm learning not to put too high a number on the limited editions," she says. "And I have many editions yet to be completed."

"Grandma Lynn's Teddybears" are available at shows, by direct mail, and from shops.

Value: They range in price from $69 to $229.

JUDI MADDIGAN

"Cubby Cousins" by Judi Maddigan is 15 inches tall and made of frosted taupe-colored German plush with guard hairs. He has a knitted suede nose, locked eyes, a sculpted mouth, shaved paw and foot pads, and stitched claws and is fully jointed. *Photo by Judi Maddigan.*

Judi Maddigan's teddies command attention because of their flair, charm, and technical expertise but above all for the open sincerity in their facial expressions.

"When I began making bears in 1984," she says, "I avoided studying other teddy bear patterns because I didn't want to be influenced by other designers. This contributed to the originality of my faces. I didn't want seams in the main face piece and designed my first bear without the

Large size (16 inches) "Chubby Cubby" by Judi Maddigan is made of German plush in "honey hug" color. He has a knitted suede nose, locked eyes, sculpted mouth, and tinted, sculpted paw and footpads. He is fully jointed and has a growler. *Photo by Judi Maddigan.*

traditional center gusset. This single, main face piece became a trademark of my designs."

Judi holds a Bachelor's degree in art, with an emphasis on design, from the University of California at Berkeley and endows her teddies with endearing extras like inset "ear wisps," two-toned ears, or sculpted toe/pad detailing and mouths. Her "Vanilla Cubcake" features a special jointing system enabling her to become either a teddy or a hand puppet.

She is not at all possessive of her innovations or patterns and has collected them in a book called *Learn Bearmaking* (Open Chain Publishing, 1989).

Judi's teddies, which range in size from 10 to 24 inches, are made of luxurious imported synthetics and have safety eyes because they are made for children.

"Even though most of my bears are owned by adults," she says, "my bears are *toys*. I specifically make their covered noses without realistic sculpting because the triangular nose immediately identifies the bear as a teddy—a toy—not a representation of a real bear. As such, they have child-safe eyes and noses. I don't use glass eyes because they are inconsistent."

Although her family sometimes helps out with the counted cross-stitch accessories or bear-size quilts the teddies hold, Judi insists on making each bear and its clothing, when used, at a rate of perhaps one a week. That is why her waiting list is eighteen months long. She sells only mail order and is an admitted perfectionist, spending ten to forty hours per bear. She averages two new designs each six months.

Value: Judi Maddigan's teddies range in price from $89 to $300.

CINDY MARTIN

❦

The Brass Bear/Yesterbears

In 1981 Cindy Martin made her first bear as a gift for her bear-collecting sister. Teaching herself, experimenting with and improving her first design, she came up with two more, this time for her daughters.

"I have never been good at following someone else's directions for doing or creating things," she says. "It's so much easier to think up ways of my own to achieve a desired effect, and more enjoyable, too."

Bearmaking soon became a lucrative means of home-based artistic expression, keeping the Fresno, California, resident close to her family. She began selling designs in 1982.

"Teddy Roosevelt Yesterbear" by Cindy Martin (© 1985) is 19 inches tall, fully jointed, and made of acrylic fur with leather paws. He wears old rimless glasses, and in his pocket he carries a watch. His outfit was made from a woollen World War II army blanket owned by Cindy's father-in-law. *Photo by Carol-Lynn Rössel Waugh.*

"Snickle" (© 1989 Cindy Martin) is a prototype made of mohair. He is 10¾ inches tall and unjointed, on a cardboard base stuffed with fiberfill. He embraces a Christmas tree. *Photo by Carol-Lynn Rössel Waugh.*

Many of Cindy's bears have heart-tugging needle-modeled faces requiring hours of redoing. With long limbs and torso, humped back, oversize paws and feet, they have an old-time, nostalgic look but are light years from antique copies. Her distinctive look is a result of constantly refining and experimenting with her first bear concept. Even in editions she resists duplication.

Her "Yesterbears" range from 3 to 58 inches in height, are fully jointed, with either leather or felt pads, and are most often made of mohair. Early bears were synthetic. Into the back of each is sewn a handwritten leather tag.

Cindy slowly hand-makes each teddy ("I seem to get slower as I go along," she says) and has cut back on production after a severe case of burnout. Although she is swamped with orders, she would never relinquish any construction steps.

"Yesterbear" by Cindy Martin (© 1982) is 23 inches tall. He is made of mohair, has leather paws, and is stuffed with fiberfill. *Photo by Carol-Lynn Rössel Waugh.*

"I want people who buy one of my bears to know that it is truly made only by me," she says, "cut out on my floor, sewn on my machine, assembled, most likely, in my bedroom. It's important to me that I keep it this way, so I can retain the style I have developed."

"Yesterbears" are seldom dressed. Cindy looks on her work as sculpture and is proud of the body shaping she has developed. Most important to her is the face.

"Eyes have to be right most of all," she says. "I want the bear to look like he is really looking into the eyes of his observer, to give the appearance of awareness, knowledge, and understanding."

"Yesterbears" are available at selected shops and directly from the artist. *Value: They range in price from $90 to $2,800.*

BARBARA McCONNELL

❧❧

McB Bears

Barbara McConnell began handcrafting teddies in April 1986 under the name "McB Bears" (her initials backward), but in a short time she was so successful that she began hiring help, and a true cottage industry employing approximately twenty women was born.

"All the women who work with us are mothers working at home in order that they may be with their children," she says. "I feel that this is very important since nowadays if I can do anything to help a mom stay at home with her kids, I will."

Barbara works from her upstairs studio, with her assistant Diane planning and designing each season's line and all of its intricate accessories.

McB Bears have an old-fashioned look, with long thin torsos, legs, and arms, and are made of fine mohair and imported fabrics. About 80% are

"Wee Bear" by Barbara McConnell, 8½ inches tall, is made of gold distressed mohair and has glass eyes. He is fully jointed and stuffed with polyester and pellets. He wears a burgundy sweater. *Photo by Carol-Lynn Rössel Waugh.*

dressed, using only the finest fabrics, usually in classic, Victorian, or fairy tale outfits. Many bears and their accessories are translations from doll concepts, and they often contain music boxes or have special extras like wardrobes and carrying cases.

They range from 7 to 28 inches in height and bear a heart-shaped stud in the left ear.

Editions range from one of a kind to 250, and Barbara has lost count of how many bears she makes annually. "I don't stop to count them," she says. "I just keep hiring more people!"

Her best-known bears are the twins Whitney and Wendy, who come in various outfits and accessories, but her antique reproduction bears and her carousel of teddies have caught the fancy of many. She also produces a line of custom-designed antique reproduction dresses for children.

As Barbara only wholesales, McB Bears are only available from shops.
Value: They range in price from $125 to $2,500.

MARGORY HOYA NOVAK

❧

Marganova

Margory Hoya Novak came to bearmaking in 1980 from the world of dolls. She still teaches porcelain dollmaking and gives workshops in bearmaking techniques when time permits. Beginning in 1973, she designed original award-winning dolls in porcelain and occasionally created plush animals to accompany them.

Her fully jointed mohair or synthetic plush teddies range in size from 7 to 24 inches and are easily indentifiable by the signed self-fabric nametag that doubles as the bear's tail. Most are undressed.

"I think it's harder to cuddle and take a dressed bear to bed with you for fear of messing it up," she says. "I like to give my bears the illusion of being dressed by using head coverings and collars, leaving their cute bare bodies soft and huggable."

Two of Marge's bears, Toby and Delia, were inspired by a *National Geographic* special on Alaska's grizzlies. "All my sketches for them were

A trio composed of 16-inch "Toby," 14-inch "Delia, the Wood Nymph," and 12-inch "Toby" is by Margory Hoya Novak. They are fully jointed and made of mohair, with glass eyes. *Photo courtesy of Margory Hoya Novak.*

Bears by Margory Hoya Novak. Back row: "Morley" (© 1986) is 16½ inches. "Tucker," right (© 1986) is 18½ inches. Seated, left, are "Gyles" (© 1988), 12½ inches, and two 9-inch "Morley" bears (© 1986). All are fully jointed, have glass eyes, and are made of mohair. *Photo courtesy of Margory Hoya Novak.*

done that day on my morning paper," she says. "The body has a rounded belly and small hump on its back while its arms are bent with paws intricately inserted, and the legs are curved in front with fetlocks in back like real bears have."

In 1988 she was selected to present two of her bears as a goodwill gesture to a delegation from the Russian "sister city" to Santa Rosa, California.

Marge has won many awards for dollmaking, and her bears have been accepted as an art form by the exclusive Sausalito, California, arts festival. But she doesn't make many of them, perhaps thirty to forty a year, with a little help in stuffing from a young friend. "An edition of three bears is big for me," she says. "Then I'm ready to move on to something else."

"Marganova" bears are available from their designer at shows or by direct mail.

Value: They range in price from $20 to $175.

NONA PEBWORTH

❦

Nona Bears

Viewing an assemblage of Nona Pebworth's teddies and reading their tags, each inscribed with the name of one of her relatives, is a bit like leafing through the pages of an ursine family album.

The bears are an apt combination of Nona's loves: genealogy, fabrics, and dolls. The Texas artist was trained as a potter but prefers working with fibers. She began making bears in the early 1980s as a way of reclaiming old quilts.

Her style can best be described as "sophisticated naiveté"; her bears, which range in size from 6 to 24 inches, combine an artist's touch with a

"Norma" by Nona Pebworth is from the artist's "Family Portrait" series. Made of 100% merino wool, she stands 15 inches tall and is dressed in a blue "sailor dress" with red tie; she wears a big blue ribbon atop her head. *Photo by Gregory Gatwright.*

charming homespun cross-eyed expression. They are a mixture of old and new, a medley of fabric surprises.

"At present," she says, "I am making bears of mohair or interesting vintage fabrics—old quilt scraps and comforters, antique fabrics and fake furs, wool and cashmere coats. They are then dressed in antique baby or doll clothes. I usually dress the bears because the thought of my bears dressed in silly clothes and wearing fake glasses (not vintage) distresses me."

"Jeffrey" by Nona Pebworth is 18 inches tall, fully jointed, and made of curly rayon fabric with safety eyes and felt pads. He is dressed in a red, white, and blue cotton knit with a mother-of-pearl belt buckle. He was made in the fall of 1987. *Photo by Gregory Gatwright.*

"Florence" by Nona Pebworth is 15 inches tall, made of mohair, and wears an old faded blue taffeta doll coat and hat with handmade lace trim. She was made in 1987. *Photo by Gregory Gatwright.*

Finally, the teddies are given family names and sometimes family garb. "Norma," she explains, "is my mother's cousin from Kansas City. And the clothing depicts her as a young schoolgirl around 1910."

In 1983 "Sarah Jane," named after two of Nona's great grandmothers, and "Ambrose," named for her grandfather, were produced in Taiwan by Faroy, Inc., of Houston, Texas, for the gift market. The following year the company marketed five more family members in synthetic fabrics.

Nona's art bears are all handmade. "I do *all* of the actual construction and finishing myself," she says. "This is a one-person studio. I do not do editions as such, and I have more ideas than I have time to carry out."

Pebworth bears are sold by appointment and at selected shows, seldom by mail. "It's hard to pick out a bear for someone else," she explains. She completes approximately 100 a year.

Value: They range in price from $60 to $295.

SARA PHILLIPS

"Faerie Bear," 1½ inches high, by Sara Phillips, is a one-of-a-kind special edition. She is adorned with lavender beads and has tiny wings. *Photo by Carol-Lynn Rössel Waugh.*

Sara Phillips's original antique-inspired jointed teddies can ride in a teaspoon and are so charming they are the prizes of many miniaturists' collections.

In 1981 the Maryland special education teacher and miniature enthusiast sought in vain true-to-scale miniature teddies for her "Teddy Bear Shop" setting, so she decided to make them. Through trial and error and a lot of research and experimentation she developed her personal style, using velour, Ultrasuède, or upholstery velvet for bodies and felt for paw pads.

Although the tallest is under 1 3/4 inches tall, most of Sara's teddies are elaborately dressed, often in soft antique trimming. Many of them boast special accessories.

A bare bear takes a minimum of eight hours to construct; a dressed bear, maybe a week.

"I'm working on refining my bears continually," Sara says, "and am always working on new designs, but I am still doing all my own work, and by hand. Unfortunately, time per bear hasn't gotten any faster over the years."

She prefers fashioning one-of-a-kind teddies, coming up with concepts such as a tiny baby bear, complete with layette and lunch, affixed to (but removable from) a dainty pillow-bed, or Victorian valentines-cum-bears.

In 1988 Sara's "Panda Clown" won a Golden Teddy award for excellence.

Nowadays she has to squeeze bearmaking around teaching and motherhood and community affairs and doesn't make many bears a year. She does absolutely no mail order or wholesale, but occasionally sells at shows and conventions.

Value: Sara Phillips's tiny teddies cost $100 and up.

"Teddy with Bear on Wheels" by Sara Phillips. "Teddy" is 1 3/4 inches tall. "Bear on Wheels" is 3/4 inch high, 1 inch long. "Teddy" is made from upholstery velvet with felt paw pads. "Bear on Wheels" is made from velour. *Photo by Carol-Lynn Rössel Waugh.*

BEVERLY MATTESON PORT

Beverly Port has been an innovator in the doll and teddy bear field since she made her first teddy bears in the 1950s. Skilled in many art forms, she has combined media since the early 1970s to produce porcelain-faced, soft-bodied dolls and teddies and is the first professional teddy bear artist of record.

In the late 1960s she introduced teddy bears as an art form in the doll world. Gradually breaking through "old guard" resistance, Bev paved the way for acceptance for subsequent waves of bearmakers, many of whom she taught and inspired.

Her articles about teddy bears and their history were published years before collecting bears became fashionable and she is well known for her lectures on the subject.

"The Wild Bear," one of the Toybox Teddies, is a FabriArt Original (© 1978-89 Beverly Matteson Port). Made of old mohair and fully jointed, he is softly stuffed and has excelsior in his paws and feet. He wears an antique-style teddy bear button on his collar. *Photo by Carol-Lynn Rössel Waugh.*

"Raggedy Muffin Cubcake," a Forgotten FabriBear (© 1987 Beverly Matteson Port), is made of vintage and recycled fabrics. Her body, upper legs, and arms are vintage pastry flour and cake sacks. Her hands have leather palms and wired separate fingers. Her head, hands, and feet are made of curly pink wool. She holds her "security bear" by the paw. She won the Golden Teddy award in 1988 and was shown at the Incorporated Gallery, New York, in 1987. *Photo by Carol-Lynn Rössel Waugh.*

Beverly's work, which bridges the gap between plaything and sculpture, has won many awards, including Golden Teddy awards, for both handmade and commercial versions and has been featured in art galleries.

She designed successful teddy bear and gift lines for Gorham-Textron from 1985 to 1988. In 1989 The House of Nisbet, Ltd. produced a yes/no version of her "co-author," Theodore B. Bear.

"Little Orphant Annie," A FabriArt Original (© 1989 Beverly Matteson Port), is made of recycled and new fabrics. Her head and lower arms are vintage distressed russet mohair. Her paws are patchwork leather signed with a red heart with a "B" patch. Her body, upper arms, and legs are from an old patterned high school sweater. Her shoes are old with oaken soles. She wears a French Provincial apron and hat and was the cover bear on the fall 1989 issue of *Teddy Bear Review* magazine. *Photo by Carol-Lynn Rössel Waugh.*

Ranging in size from 1 inch to life size, Beverly's repertoire ranges from fantasy bears to high-fashion teddies with swivel waists and armatured arms to mechanical bears and nostalgic "Time Machine Teddies," who wear her well-known medallion with the logo: "Won't you be my Teddy Bear?" Others are trademarked with a "Bee" for "Bearverly."

Many Port designs are musical; some contain secret compartments or feature unexpected juxtapositions of fibers and ideas, such as patchwork leather paws or underbodies made of cake sacks, sweaters, or recycled memorabilia.

Because Bev works slowly, does all of her work alone, and is always experimenting, her production is very limited and her waiting list is lengthy. Her teddies are occasionally available by direct mail or through Emily's Cottage in Bremerton, Washington, and other select stores.

Value: Beverly Port Originals range in price from $295 to $5,000.

JOHN PAUL PORT

John Paul Port was born into a family of bearmakers and made his first teddy bear as a Christmas gift for his parents in 1975. In 1979 he devised a no/no bear for his sister Kim's birthday. But he made his "selling" debut as a bearmaker in January 1988.

"Tiger Lily," © 1988 John Paul Port, is approximately 9 inches tall. She is fully jointed, made of white mohair, has twinkling black eyes, and embroidered nose, mouth, and claws. *Photo by Carol-Lynn Rössel Waugh.*

John's fully jointed mohair bears, which are often sold under the "Van Poort and Company" banner (Van Poort being the family's original name) are at times trademarked with a windmill, at times with a gold metallic Dutch boy, and range in size from 3 1/2 to 28 inches tall.

Perhaps the most readily identifiable of John's bears are his often imitated flower bears," little teddies with names such as "Miss Tulip," "Daffadilly," and "Tiger Lily" wearing hats made from artificial flowers. These are an offspin of his innovative series of photographs of teddies in flower gardens. He is an avid teddy bear photographer whose work has appeared in print and has been shown in slides at bear conventions throughout the country.

An expert on antique bears from an early age, John is often called on to appraise and identify bears. He writes a column about his adventures tracking down elderly teddies called "The Bear Sleuth" for *Teddy Bear Review* magazine and owns a shop, with its own "bear corner," called Emily's Cottage, named for his mother's bear, "Miss Emily."

"Mama Memoree" by John Paul Port is made of mohair, fully jointed, and stuffed with polyester. She is approximately 18 inches tall. *Photo by Carol-Lynn Rössel Waugh.*

"Patches and Stitches" by John Paul Port are approximately 7 inches tall. These children of "Mama Memoree" are made of mohair, are fully jointed, and "were played with so much they are mended and patched." *Photo by Carol-Lynn Rössel Waugh.*

Most of John's bears are undressed. His largest edition is fifty pieces; most are one of a kind. He does all of his work alone, and his output is very limited.

Value: John Paul Port's teddy bears range in price from $65 to $500.

KIMBERLEE PORT

Kimbearlee Kreations™

When Kimberlee Port began making bears in 1974, she was an anomaly. Few people made art bears then, and fewer still made miniatures. But bears were a family concern, and Kim came up with her first original that year as a Christmas present for her mom. She was fourteen. By the time she was sixteen, her family of Christmas teddies had graced the cover of *Doll News*, receiving national acclaim.

"Bearquet the Bearterfly," © 1988 Kimberlee Port, made of rust mohair, has a torso embellished with ribbon embroidery technique. The vintage ribbon flowers are also handmade. She is approximately 6 inches tall, including her handpainted, soft yellow wings. *Photo by Carol-Lynn Rössel Waugh.*

"Little Gold" (© 1984-89 Kimberlee Port) is 2 inches tall, fully jointed, and made of mohair with felt paw pads. She is dressed in vintage ribbon. *Photo by Carol-Lynn Rössel Waugh.*

Her work, which has won many awards, including the Golden Teddy award, has been displayed in several art galleries, including the Incorporated Gallery in New York City, and was on permanent display at the London Doll and Toy Museum. She is widely known for the entertaining cooking column she writes for *Teddy Bear Review* magazine and for the seminars she gives at bear conventions.

Always an innovator, Kim consistently produces designs stretching the definition of "teddy bearness," introducing such subsequently imitated concepts as "bearterflies," "Fleur" (a flower bear), and "Teddy, Teddy Tree," a green mohair Christmas tree bear with working miniature ornaments and "teddy star" on top. The latter has no precedent, antique or modern.

The first artist of record to create tiny, full jointed teddies as an art form, her work ranges in size between ¹/₂ and 21 inches tall.

This long-nosed "Old Fashioned Teddy" (© Kimberlee Port) is approximately 3 inches tall, fully jointed, and made of gold low-pile fabric. *Photo by Carol-Lynn Rössel Waugh.*

Kim is renowned for using the seamline joining body pieces in her smallest teddies as a design element. These entail from nineteen to thirty-four individual minute fabric pieces and hundreds of tiny hand stitches. Larger teddies have turned pieces.

Because of the slow, painstaking way in which she creates her work, Kim's editions never exceed ten bears. She produces fewer than fifty annually. They are easily recognizable by their appealing faces ("I often spend four to five hours just on the face, to get the expression right," she says) and by their outstanding workmanship and attention to details. All of Kim's bears sport a signed clear-plastic heart; she was the first bear artist to use a heart as her signature. Some of her tiny teddies come in custom-made boxes designed to complement their contents.

"Kimbearlee Kreations"℠ are available directly from the artist, occasionally from shops or at shows.

Value: They range in price from $150 to $950.

CYNTHIA POWELL

🎀

Bearly Bears

Cynthia Powell began making teddies early in 1987 because it was hard to find bears under $3\frac{1}{2}$ inches for her collection.

A gemologist with a degree in fine art and a former jewelry designer, she had the skills and the inspiration to make them, but it took six months to perfect techniques and patterns.

Although her teddies range in size from a mere $\frac{1}{2}$ inch to 3 inches, Cynthia packs a lot of wonder into them. Many of her favorites contain special surprises like compacts or purses or perfume bottles. Her sailor bear hides a compass inside.

"I try to bring back some of childhood's delights," she says. "They say

"Compact Bear" by Cynthia Powell, $2\frac{1}{4}$ inches tall, is made of hand-dyed lavender fabric. He opens to reveal a tiny compact with powder concealed within. *Photo by Carol-Lynn Rössel Waugh.*

Cynthia Powell's 1 3/4-inch unjointed bear of plush nylon fabric stuffed with fiberfill and dried lavender wears old-fashioned doll clothes. She has miniature straw baskets sewn to her dress and stitched leather shoes. She comes with her own zippered carrying case with accessories. *Photo by Carol-Lynn Rössel Waugh.*

'kicks' just keep getting harder to get. Well, I still get them by creating my bears."

One of her most delightful is "dolly bear," who comes in a suitcase full of accessories.

Cynthia's originals are fashioned from nineteen to forty pieces each and she hand-sews them all, working on off hours maybe three days a week. The bears themselves are made from a plush fabric with a tightly woven backing. Eyes are hand-painted brass. Clothing is often an integral part of the bear's body or is sewn from antique or modern silk, linen, or cotton fabrics and trimmings.

Cynthia produces around seventy-five bears annually, most of them in

"Teddy Trinket and Baby Clown" by Cynthia Powell are 2½ inches and 1¼ inches respectively. Of plush nylon fabric, they are stuffed with fiberfill. "Teddy Trinket" is actually a coin purse disguised as a bear. *Photo by Carol-Lynn Rössel Waugh.*

editions of less than twenty. Many are one of a kind. Her bears can be obtained by mail order, at the few shows she attends, or from "The Owl and the Pussycat" in Ft. Myers, Florida, or "Kits and Kaboodle," in Indianapolis, Indiana.

Value: They range in price from $75 to $225.

JANET REEVES

❦

Hug-a-Bear

Janet Reeves, a former art major, has a preference for three-dimensional art and design, including sculpting, ceramics, and wood carving. She says her bearmaking, which began in 1985, is a natural progression.

Janet's bears range in size from 6½ to 22 inches, but most are 10 to 14 inches tall. She is perhaps best known for her teddy "Lida Rose" and also for the unusual combinations of colors she uses: lavender-tipped mohair or off-white with mauve pads and nose.

"Lucy Locket" by Janet Reeves is made of light beige mohair with Ultrasuède paw pads and glass eyes, she is 13½ inches tall and stuffed with polyester fiberfill. Her dress is light rose with small white flowers, and around her neck is a locket. Limited edition of 200. *Photo by Warner Photography.*

Only about 20% of Janet's teddies are dressed; she believes most collectors, like her, prefer them bare.

Janet tries to create bears with all of the traditional characteristics of old teddies and pays attention to fine detail. She does all design and construction work; her husband cuts joints and bear parts, her daughter stuffs arms and legs.

Edition size per bear ranges from 75 to 500; an average edition is 100 to 200 bears. In 1988 she made about 700 teddies in her woodland home in rural Michigan.

"Hug-a-Bear" teddies can be purchased from shops nationwide, at shows, and by direct mail.

Value: They range in price from $65 to $250.

BETSY L. REUM

Bears-in-the-Gruff

"Priscilla" and "Penny Fairy" by Betsy Reum are 14 and 6 inches tall, respectively. "Priscilla" is made of off-white wavy plush. "Penny Fairy" is costumed in white, pink, and silver and holds a gold magic wand. *Photo by Kim Kauffman*.

While at Michigan State University, Betsy Reum studied clothing and textiles, including pattern-making skills and design techniques. In 1981 she chose to use her training making crafts, enabling her to stay at home with her young son. She quickly discovered that a little velour bear, named Wellington, adapted from a commercial pattern, was a best-seller.

By 1985 she had designed her first original in acrylic; in November 1986, her first mohair bear, "Toby," was born.

Betsy's current line debuted in September 1987 with her logo bear and first limited edition, "The Puppeteer," complete with strolling "Punch and Judy" show.

Today Betsy specializes in bears dressed in nostalgic, turn-of-the-century costumes, such as "The Postman," who has innovative thumbs enabling him to hold letters, and "The Parlor Maid," wearing a traditional black dress. About 75% of Betsy's production is dressed. They range in size from 5 to 16 inches.

Betsy embroiders unusual noses, with shaped nostrils, on newer bears. They have been signed, since October 1988, on the underside of their ultasuede-lined tails. She does most of the work herself, relying occasionally on help for cutting, machining, stuffing, and costume construction. All bears are numbered per pattern, regardless of color, and are limited to 500. She produces 250 teddies a year.

"Bears-in-the-Gruff" are available by direct mail, at three or four shows annually, and nationwide from approximately fifteen bear shops.

Value: They range in price from $80 to $230.

GLORIA ROSENBAUM

❧

Rosenbear Designs Ltd.

"Elizabeth Ann Rosenbear," designed by Gloria Rosenbaum, is 20 inches tall, fully jointed, and made of light antique-gold distressed German mohair. She has dimpled, bent knees and wears Battenberg lace panties with diaper, booties, bonnet and collar. She holds a silver-coated pewter dumbbell rattle. *Photo by Carol-Lynn Rössel Waugh.*

When Gloria Rosenbaum designed her first original teddy bear in 1986, it was a quest for self-sufficiency and artistic expression. She had been "let go" from a government job for health reasons and was determined to make it on her own.

A stint on the crafts circuit with soft-sculptured dolls led her to explore bearmaking, which soon grew into a profitable business.

Gloria's early teddies, inspired by dollmaking successes, were notable for their elaborate glitzy clothing and felt eyelids. Today's bears, while still dressed, possess distinct personalities and are more "old-fashioned" looking. Aimed at a decidedly upscale clientele, they wear the finest of fabrics and trimmings and come with story lines. All sport a trademarked fabric rose in the right ear.

Made of mohair or fine synthetics, they range in size from 10 to 36 inches. Most are fully jointed.

Although Gloria still makes prototypes and oversees production, her teddies have grown so popular (forty or fifty are shipped out a week) that she has formed a cottage industry to produce them. Fifteen home workers—cutters, jointers, hand-sewers, and stuffers—combine efforts to produce Rosenbears. Her husband, Mike, helps with finishing work and management.

Gloria has won awards, including Golden Teddy awards, for Rosenbears and has been called on to design for other companies.

She only wholesales, and her work is available in shops in the United States and abroad.

Value: "Rosenbear Designs Ltd." teddies range in price from $90 to $650.

KATHY SANDUSKY

❦

Sandusky's Bear Cupboard

Kathy Sandusky, who has been sewing since childhood, began making bears in 1983.

They range in size from 7 to 20 inches, are fully jointed, made of mohair, and have glass eyes.

Sandusky Bears are easily recognizable by their kind, gentle expressions. Perhaps Kathy's best-known bear is "The Happy Wanderer."

Kathy and her husband, Owen, do all of the bearmaking. Occasionally, they have some help with clothing. About one quarter of their teddies are dressed.

Annual production is about 350 bears, which can be purchased by direct mail, at shows, or from teddy bear shops.

Value: Sandusky bears range in price from $55 to $225.

"Gretchen" by Kathy Sandusky is 20 inches tall and made of beige distressed mohair. Fully jointed and stuffed with polyester fiberfill, she wears an antique baby dress. *Photo courtesy of Kathy Sandusky.*

LAURIE SASAKI

❦

The Bearrie Patch

"Bearrie Patch Marching Band Member" by Laurie Sasaki was made in 1986, one of an edition of ten sets. The drummer bear is 4½ inches high and made of upholstery fabric. The uniform, with its blue jacket, is an integral part of his gray body. *Photo courtesy of Laurie Sasaki.*

Although her bears have at times reached 19 inches in height since she began making them full-time in 1985, native Californian Laurie Sasaki specializes in miniature bears, 4 inches and under. The smallest of these is 1½ inches tall.

"I strive to achieve such perfect proportion and detail in my miniature teddies," she says, "that, without a scale reference, they might be mistaken for their larger counterparts."

Working alone in her two-bedroom apartment, she spends an average of eight hours on each completely hand-sewn bear, producing 150 to 200 annually. Most styles are unlimited; "editions" range from ten to fifty.

"I design each new size and style of bear completely from scratch," she says. "I never reduce or enlarge existing patterns to create a new bear. Most of my designs differ radically from one another."

But Sasaki bears show a consistency of expression that makes them recognizable as her work, and the embroidered paw pads of her 2 1/4-inch tall bears and bunnies make them immediately identifiable.

Only 20% of her bears are "dressed." Actually, their "clothing" is an integral part of their bodies and not removable.

"Chester" and "Buster" by Laurie Sasaki are 19 and 13 inches respectively. These bears are fully jointed, and made of mohair. "Chester" has black glass eyes and features a center seam in his head. *Photo courtesy of Laurie Sasaki.*

Two miniature bears by Laurie Sasaki, made in 1987, are 2¼ inches tall. Each bear is fully jointed, made of synthetic velvet upholstery fabric, and has black bead eyes and an embroidered nose and mouth. The bear in the foreground is gold; the one in background is beige. *Photo courtesy of Laurie Sasaki.*

Laurie's bears are available from her only at shows. She does not sell to shops and will not answer mail inquiries. "I have learned from experience," she says. "This is the only way I can operate. For me, filling orders takes away the joy I feel in making bears, and the pressure puts a damper on my creative energy. Above all, if I were to fill orders I would never have enough bears to do the shows, and I would miss all the fun of traveling and meeting other bear artists and collectors."

Value: "Bearrie Patch" bears range in price from $75 to $175.

MARIA SCHMIDT

❧

The Charlestowne Bear

Maria Schmidt graduated from Central Michigan State University in 1979 with an honors BFA in ceramic art and sculpture. She has been making bears since 1983 and specializes in large, superbly crafted bears reminiscent of old Steiffs but far more durable.

"My bears are a piece of art meant to be loved," she says. "They look so much happier and have much more character if they are handled often.

"Kodi" by Maria Schmidt was made in 1988 of 1-inch-long honey-colored mohair. He is fully jointed and stuffed with fiberfill. *Photo courtesy of Maria Schmidt.*

I recommend hugging and playing with them as much as possible. Don't just put them on a shelf. That's what the *antique* bears are for!"

Although she has made 8-inch-high teddies, most of them stand at least 2 feet tall, some over 38 inches. And none is ever clothed.

"I don't really care for dressed bears," Maria says. "I feel it hides the sculptured shape of the bear. To me a bear isn't just a pretty face but a beautiful body too! My bear's personality is created through giving the bear 'presence.' He looks as if he's 'in there.' My bears do not look off into space but at you. They have pleasant faces and a look that reveals a soul inside. I detest bears that just sit there like a stuffed toy."

Maria puts ten to twelve hours into each bear and often redoes her teddies until they meet her strict standards. Averaging fewer than 25 bears a year, she does all the work herself.

"I think that all artist-made bears should be *totally* made by the artist," she says. "If they have help in the sewing or stuffing, call them something else or give the helper full credit."

She no longer takes orders and sells her bears at only one or two shows a year.

Value: "The Charlestowne Bear" ranges in price from $200 to $1500.

STEVE SCHUTT

❧

Bear-"S"-Ence

One of the best respected and most original contemporary teddy bear artists, Steve Schutt credits growing up in Iowa with allowing his artistic talents to develop.

"Iowa is a place to grow," he says. "There aren't the pressures and fast pace of city life. And my parents did such a good job of encouraging me to try whatever caught my fancy."

Until 1983 he experimented with many media, from *Pyssansky* (Ukrain-

"Cornelius, the Coal Miner" by Steve Schutt is 24 inches tall. *Photo by Ron Kimball.*

ian Easter eggs) to quiltmaking, and even managed an antiques store.
Finally, all the threads tied together; drawing on his 25 years of puppetry
experience and antiques expertise, Steve began making bears.

Early adaptive efforts, created of horsehair, old coverlets, feedsacks,
garage sale coats, and mohair from old sofas gave way to innovative experiments with size, concept, and style. In 1985 Steve attended the first
American Teddy Bear Artist Guild convention. This put him in touch with
mainstream artists and collectors and his work "took off."

Today a Steve Schutt bear, marketed under the 'Bear-S-Ence" label, is
immediately recognizable by both its facial expression (Steve says it's vital
for his bears to have "soul") and its flair. His work has won coveted Golden
Teddy awards.

Basically a one-man operation, Steve makes fewer than 200 bears a
year but has so many orders he has hired a seamstress to machine the
mohair and all nonantique clothes for his tall, elongated bruins. "When I
use antique clothes," he says, "I alter the bear to fit the clothing, not the
other way around."

Each of the Schutt bears, which range in size from 5 1/2 inches to over

"Silas," 36 inches tall, is by Steve Schutt. *Photo by Ron Kimball.*

Steve Schutt's mohair panda is 26 inches tall. *Photo by Ron Kimball.*

3 feet tall, is identifiable by the metal stud embossed with "SS" attached to the back of its head, and by its nose stitching: a narrow horizontal rectangle ending in a slight smile.

Schutt bears are sold only at shows by the artist (absolutely no mail order) and at three select shops. Some, such as his experiments with cross-breeding dinosaurs and bears or his large attenuated bruins, are closer to sculpture. Others, pot-bellied and huggable, are closer to toys or childhood companions.

All are sensitive, artistic statements reflecting the personality of their creator.

Value: "Bear-S-Ence" bears range in price from $100 to more than $3,000.

CHRISTINE SHELTERS

❧

Bears by Christine

Golden tan "Humphrey" by Christine Shelters, in 18-inch size, is made of mohair, has glass eyes, and is fully jointed. *Photo by Carol-Lynn Rössel Waugh.*

Christine Shelters's teddies probably have the most readily recognizable "noses and toeses" in the business.

She designed her bears' feet so that they arch in from the edges to a center dimple from which her "claw" stitching emerges. This depression-arch allows her teddies to balance in even the largest sizes, unaided by bear stands.

Her bears' noses are slowly built up, with layer after layer of crewel stitches, into a solid shape of thread that looks almost as if it could smell honey.

Christine's bears are almost always unembellished, never gimmicky. Occasionally, she will dress one as an elf or a fairy, but it is always evident that underneath the costume stands a wise and knowing bear.

Her style is classic, her faces expressive, her changes and evolutions of patterns subtle; she excels in contouring the body into a "real bear" posture. She uses only mohair, alpaca, and wool in "real bear" hues.

Christine's bears stand from 8 to 30 inches; being an artist who does best with a "large canvas," her large bears are her masterpieces.

Soft-spoken and retiring in nature, she rarely attends shows, preferring to sell her bears through selected shops. Her annual production varies, depending on the size of bear: perhaps five a week. A purist, she insists on totally making each teddy.

Value: "Bears by Christine" range in price from $135 to $750.

MARCIA SIBOL

❦

Bar Harbor Bears

Marcia Sibol's elegantly dressed lady bears are the end product of a lifelong love affair with the needle.

"Hildy" by Marcia Sibol (1989) is a slender, 20-inch-tall young lady with old shoe button eyes. Made of distressed gold mohair, she wears a straw hat and high-top shoes. She is dressed in homespun-type cottons, and her muslin apron has a hand-quilted bib. *Photo by Carol-Lynn Rössel Waugh*.

"Alice" by Marcia Sibol is 22 inches tall. This parasol-toting champagne mohair lady wears a blue satin gown with bodice and lower sleeves inset with hand-beaded lace. Her bustle is trimmed with silk flowers, and her lace-covered hat is trimmed with tulle bows, silk flowers, baby's-breath, and lovebirds. *Photo by Carol-Lynn Rössel Waugh.*

Re-creating and studying Paris originals led her to a career in custom dressmaking for both people and antique dolls.

Somewhere along the way Marcia began making soft-sculpted toys, including thread-jointed bears. When, in 1982, she showed one to her friend, Tom Tear, who was then making elaborate gowns for bears, he encouraged her to make a "properly jointed bear." Both her Senior Bear, "Barnaby," and a bearmaking partnership were born.

For awhile Tom and Marcia both made bears under the "Bar Harbor Bears" logo. Now Marcia carries on alone, making bears ranging in height from 8 to 24 inches, working with the same professionalism as when she garbed beauty pageant contestants.

"My goal is quality, not quantity," Marcia says, "and I do all the work myself."

Marcia's fully jointed mohair bears, whether traditional soft-stuffed teddies, children in Liberty cottons and Pendleton woolens, or elegant slim-waisted ladies wearing hand-beaded couture, are notable for meticulous attention to detail, which has won many prizes, including a Golden Teddy award.

Value: "Bar Harbor Bears" cost between $100 and $750.

BARBARA SIXBY

❧

Zücker Bears

"Calvin" by Barbara Sixby is 18 inches tall, made of distressed mohair, and fully jointed. *Photo courtesy of Barbara Sixby.*

Barbara Sixby began making bears at age 17. In 1989 she had been making bears for seven years and was married to the man for whom she made her first teddy.

Over the years, Barbara's "Zücker Bears" have evolved, as any artist's work will, always retaining their hallmark pizzazz and insouciance.

"I think that if you have a sense of style, your work will be recognizable," she says. "I like all my bears to have big noses, smiles, and close-set eyes. I try to create bears that look as if they are trying to talk. And I want them to be caricatures. If a bear is too serious, I will redo the face until I am satisfied."

Perhaps Barbara's best-known innovation is her early use of the yes/

no mechanism. She delights in constantly changing her line, ranging in size from 3 to 36 inches tall.

"The process of evolution from paper to a three-dimensional object is exciting to me," she says. "I see nothing wrong with seeing an idea and then interpreting it and making it your own. But to copy verbatim makes me annoyed. I think there is an unlimited amount of ideas, and everyone should strive to make his creations unique."

Although she reluctantly will make specially commissioned bears, Barbara does not do editions, nor has she any idea of how many bears she and her mother make. Her mom is her partner and does all the finishing work. Barbara does the sewing and the face on each "Zücker" bear.

Barbara supplies bears to many shops and attends shows throughout the year. She also sells mail order.

Value: "Zücker Bears" range in price from $75 to $800.

JAN SMALL

❧

Jan Small's Heirloom Bears

Jan Small creates her endearingly worried-miened teddies in what she terms "the bear factory" at the rear of the art gallery she owns in Harlingen, Texas. "I used to have a room at home I called the factory," she says, "but this is more businesslike."

Jan's first original bear, Horatio, made on a creative whim in late 1985, was accepted for the 1987 Workman Teddy Bear Calendar and created such a demand that Jan decided to become a bearmaker. Today she handmakes approximately 400 originals annually, ranging in size from 7½ to over 30 inches, in editions of fifty each.

Her "Hermione" won a Golden Teddy award in 1987.

Perhaps Jan's best-known teddy is 30-inch tall "Hugh Mongus," whom she describes as "a companion, a protector, a piece of furniture in his own right."

"Maisie" by Jan Small (1989) is 11 inches tall and made of mohair. *Photo by Jan Small.*

"Three Be-Sweatered Henrys" by Jan Small (1989) are mohair bears, 14 inches tall. *Photo by Jan Small.*

Most are undressed, except for an occasional sweater knitted to order. "I like the look of hairier bears," she says, "and prefer bare bears to dressed ones. But a sweater seems the most natural garment for a teddy if he has to have one."

They are fully jointed, made of fine mohair and synthetics, and brimming with personality.

"My bears are changing," she says. "The look is becoming sillier, more whimsical, I think."

Jan Small's Heirloom Teddies are available directly from her and through selected shops.

Value: They range in price from $75 to $400.

LINDA SPIEGEL

Bearly There

"Smoochie" by "Bearly There," designed by Linda Spiegel, is 5½ inches tall and made of distressed mohair with felt pads, wooden black bead eyes, and brown floss nose and claws. He is partially stuffed to give the slumpy appearance of an old bear. *Photo by John Limbocker/Limbo Vision.*

Linda Spiegel, who has been sewing since she was four, started her "Bearly There" company in her garage in 1980. While raising her family of six, for a period of twelve years, she had made dresses and accessories for antique dolls, so teddy bear making seemed a logical business to undertake.

In 1983 Linda and her partners had grown so successful she moved to a commercial building. Today "Bearly There" has twelve regular and five seasonal employees, all of them women, some of whom were unskilled and living on welfare but who now can afford their own homes.

Today Linda does little hands-on work; she designs the bears and is the creative force behind the company, and she travels extensively, as far away as Japan, to promote it. And the ladies in Westminster, California, produce her designs in regular editions of 200 bears each or special editions of 500. They also do contract work for other bear artists and will produce designs to order.

Linda's bears, from 5½ to 32 inches tall, are easily recognizable by their expressions, from her early "Silly Basil" to the popular "Spanky" and "Gus." The company has 140 different items on its line, including approximately 80 or 90 new bears a year.

About half are dressed. Linda carefully researches and responds to the marketplace, since she sells only wholesale to shops in the United States and abroad.

Value: "Bearly There" bears range in price from $35 to $250.

KATHLEEN WALLACE

❦

Stier Bears

Kathleen Wallace began making bears in 1984 as a hobby, using commercial patterns until she learned the mechanics of bear design. Her goal was to create teddies evoking characteristics of the antiques she loved. She sold at local craft shows, constantly revising her designs until, in 1987, she felt she was ready for the competition of national bear shows.

Kathleen's "Stier Bears" have a gentle, old-fashioned look, often a center-seamed head, and a beautiful, gentle expression speaking well of the time she spent developing them and inviting favorable comparisons with

Made of cinnamon-colored distressed mohair, this 16-inch-tall, fully jointed teddy with glass eyes wears an old medal. He was made by Kathleen and Jim Wallace. *Photo by Carol-Lynn Rössel Waugh.*

old Steiffs, especially when they are garbed in antique or reproduction period clothing. Most of the time Kathleen is reluctant to cover their mohair bodies; her customers prefer them "bare."

Bearmaking has become a full-time business for Kathleen, her husband Jim, and their family. Together, in 1988, they made 700 teddies, from 9 to 43 inches tall. Most editions are around 75 bears, but the Wallaces have a general line in which 50 bears each is produced.

The family attends fifteen shows a year, sells wholesale, and has opened a shop in Churchtown, Pennsylvania, in the heart of Amish country. "What a wonderful life this venture has created for us!" Kathleen says.

Value: "Stier Bears" range in price from $80 to $495.

CAROL-LYNN RÖSSEL WAUGH

"Jessica," 22 inches tall, is fully jointed and made of long honey-colored German mohair, with cotton velveteen paw pads and glass eyes. She was designed on Thanksgiving 1988 and wears a heart-shaped pendant (© Carol-Lynn Rössel Waugh). *Photo by Carol-Lynn Rössel Waugh.*

Carol-Lynn Rössel Waugh (the co-author of this book) grew up in New York City loving dolls, art, and books and has made them her life's work. She taught herself to sew doll and teddy bear clothes at six, designing originals at an early age, and went on to earn two degrees in the history of art.

A prolific writer, mystery anthologist, and award-winning photographer, the Winthrop, Maine, resident is adept in many media, from watercolors to sculpture. She is best known in the doll and teddy bear worlds for her many photo-illustrated books and articles chronicling the work of contemporary artists. She is also an internationally respected teddy bear designer, producing work for three commercial firms as well as handmade originals for collectors.

A self-taught award-winning doll artist, she made her first jointed "teddy bear dolls" of porcelain in the mid-1970s, graduating to latex composition in the 1980s.

Her first mohair design, "Yetta Nother Bear," made in September 1985, was produced commercially by the House of Nisbet, Ltd. in 1987 and was

"Hanna's Sister," 15 inches tall, is fully jointed and made of curly German mohair with velveteen paw pads and glass eyes. She wears a heart-shaped pendant and a contented expression; designed in 1988 (© Carol-Lynn Rössel Waugh). *Photo by Carol-Lynn Rössel Waugh.*

"L'ilbears," © Carol-Lynn Rössel Waugh 1989, are made of upholstery fabric with cotton velveteen paw pads and metallic heart necklaces. They stand $2^5/8$ and 3 inches tall and have metal joints. *Left to right.* "Pink Tink Tinkerbear" (rosy pink with gray paw pads) and "L'ilguy" (honey color with brown paw pads). *Photo by Carol-Lynn Rössel Waugh.*

a best-seller, leading to other designs, including a yes/no bear named "Maybe." Her successful work for Effanbee Dolls ("Gilda and Gordon") has further proved her versatility in the commercial marketplace.

Carol-Lynn's originals range in size from 2 to 22 inches, are fully jointed, and distinguished by their sensitive, intelligent expressions, derived through a combination of needle sculpture and embroidery. Most have contented smiles and prominent noses. All sport distinctive embroidered eyebrows and wear a heart-shaped pendant around the neck. Most of her collector bears, as opposed to her commercial work, are undressed.

Because she is primarily a writer/photographer and because she works very slowly, believing an artist's bear should be completely handmade by its designer, Carol-Lynn's annual production is usually less than fifty teddies. That is why she has designed for home crafters an ongoing line of patterns for making bears and clothing centering on "Yetta Nother Bear" and her extensive family. Bears and patterns are available directly; selected shops infrequently carry Waugh teddies. Carol-Lynn also sells at two or three shows a year.

Value: Carol-Lynn Rössel Waugh's originals range in price from $100 to $1,000.

APRIL WHITCOMB-GUSTAFSON

April Whitcomb-Gustafson has always approached bearmaking as an art form. A full-time art director with a B.A. in art education, she is an accomplished painter. And the little bears she creates are articulated sculpture.

"I have to categorize my bears as sculpture," she says, "for it is the sculpture I do that gives the bear the basis for its expression."

April sculpts these 2-inch teddies of clay, then covers them with velveteens and other luxurious low-nap fabrics to simulate plush. She paints their features and strings them like porcelain dolls. When appropriate, she costumes them in to-scale, accurate, effective, and whimsical nonremovable fashions.

Portrait bear of Bill Gustafson, husband of April Whitcomb-Gustafson, its maker; a one-of-a-kind bear. *Photo courtesy of April Whitcomb-Gustafson.*

April hand-makes each teddy in an edition of fifty. Her mom enhances them with beautiful theme-related, fabric-covered boxes, and her dad fashions wooden props.

Since 1981 she has created character bears and fantasy creatures and teddy dioramas, such as a reenactment of the Clifford Berryman cartoon depicting Theodore Roosevelt and the bear he refused to shoot or an organ grinder bear with "monkey" bear on leash, complete with handmade wooden organ. The latter won the Golden Teddy award and was shown at New York's Incorporated Gallery.

"Teddy Roosevelt and the Bear" by April Whitcomb-Gustafson won first prize at the ATBAG convention in Boston in 1987. *Photo courtesy of April Whitcomb-Gustafson.*

"The Organ Grinder" by April Whitcomb-Gustafson won a Golden Teddy award in 1987. *Photo courtesy of April Whitcomb-Gustafson.*

"I aim for people who really appreciate fine detail and imaginative design for the discriminating collector who collects only the top of the line," she says.

From 1985 to 1988 April was associate designer for the House of Nisbet in England, during which time they produced 10-inch tall adaptations of three of her bears. But her sculpted teddies, especially her one-of-a-kind commissions, are available only from her.

Value: They range in price from $100 to $1,000.

BONNIE WINDELL

❧❀❧

Windlewood

"Shoo" by Bonnie Windell is 7 inches tall, fully jointed, and made of mohair with glass eyes. He wears cotton ticking overalls and a brown hat with earholes. A fly perches permanently on his nose; he holds a flyswatter in one paw. *Photo by Carol-Lynn Rössel Waugh.*

Bonnie Windell claims she "discovered" Windlewood, where her original teddies live, in 1987 while walking in the woods surrounding her southern Indiana home.

Although she has no formal art training, she began sewing for her dolls and stuffed animals in childhood and has always loved and collected dolls. Her first attempt at bearmaking was for a contest from a commercial pattern. She soon began designing her own teddies, now ranging in size from 5 to 14 inches.

Besides bears, she designs possums, dogs, and mice: all the creatures inhabiting Windlewood.

Bonnie's bears are traditional-looking; about half are dressed because, she says, "clothing lends a personality and a sense of humor to them."

Bonnie's bear "Shoo," flyswatter in paw, fly permanently perched on his nose, is a good example of this.

Bonnie does all the work herself with a little help in cutting-out from her son. She sets no limit on her editions, which may be bought by mail, from shops, or shows.

Value: "Windlewood" bears range in price from $99 to $350.

PAMELA SUE WOOLEY

✿

Wooley Bear Cottage

Pamela Sue Wooley's undergraduate studies in fine art and sociology and her love for antiques combined in 1984 when she began making teddy bears.

Ranging in size from 5 to 32 inches, made of the finest imported materials, "Wooley Bear Cottage" teddies are easily recognizable by their softly padded ears giving the impression they may hear you.

Pamela spends ten to twelve hours handcrafting each teddy. "I do all the work myself," she says. "I refuse to be part of a 'family factory' because

"Radcliffe" by Pamela Wooley is 22 inches tall and has suede pads and glass eyes. He is made from long, extra-dense rust-colored mohair and has softly stuffed deeply set ears. *Photo by Carol-Lynn Rössel Waugh.*

that is not the way an 'artist bear' is made, even if it was originally designed by an artist."

She prides herself on meticulous workmanship and often spends two hours clipping the faces of her teddies to produce their expressions, reminiscent of early American Ideal teddies.

"Expressions are everything," she says. "And my bears have gorgeous expressions. And they're finished to perfection."

Only about one-third of Pamela's bears are dressed; most wear, instead of clothing, antique handmade lace collars from the mid-1800s or starched white menswear collars from the early 1900s with original collar buttons and vintage bow ties. Sometimes special collectors' editions are clothed but never overclothed. Some bears carry antique pocket watches or wear wire-rimmed glasses. Girls may wear antique sterling silver hearts.

Many "Wooley Bear Cottage" teddies are one of a kind; limited editions number 50 or 100, and all are made to order. Pamela produces 300 bears a year, which can be purchased by direct mail, at shops, or at shows.

Value: "Wooley Bear Cottage" bears range in price from $120 to $695.

BEVERLY MARTIN WRIGHT

❦

The Wright Bears

This 13-inch honey-colored mohair bear, made in 1987 by Beverly Martin Wright, has jointed limbs, a swivel head, Plexiglass eyes, hand-embroidered nose, synthetic suede paw pads, and a sweater designed and made by Bev Wright. *Photo by Ron Kimball.*

Beverly Martin Wright majored in art in school, studied sculpture at the Art Institute of San Francisco, and has privately studied numerous arts and crafts, particularly fiber arts. She made her first jointed bear in 1980, with instruction and encouragement from her niece, Lynda Carswell, who had been making bears since 1973.

For awhile they made and sold bears together as "Heirloom Bears," following the crafts circuit in the San Francisco area until Beverly perfected her own designs in 1983 and began selling them under the "Wright Bears" banner.

"I begin a design," Bev says, "with a mental image, then pattern templates, a trial bear, pattern changes, and then a prototype. I've never spent more than eight hours on a design."

Beverly's fully jointed Plexiglass-eyed bears have lovely symmetry and a readily identifiable perky expression; the mohair on their heads usually runs "upward." Her noses have extra stitching, giving them a slightly sculpted look.

They range in size from 6 to 24 inches; most are between 11 and 15 inches tall. About half are dressed in hand-knit cable sweaters; older bears had clothing Beverly no longer has time to make.

"I operate a one-person workshop," she says. "I'm president, shipping clerk, bookkeeper, and janitor. I do all the work on every bear, including the sweater knitting. Why? I live in a remote place and haven't found the right person yet but long for someone to work with me."

Beverly's editions range from 40 to 300 teddies; Bev makes about 450 bears a year, available only from shops.

Value: "The Wright Bear" ranges in price from $90 to $175.

NAN WRIGHT

Olde Tyme Toys & Treasures

"John Paul" by Nan Wright is 22 inches high, fully jointed, and made of fawn brown imported synthetic. He has a brown lambskin leather nose and paws and soft brown glass eyes. He is signed "Nanc" on a paw pad with a branding iron. *Photo by Carol-Lynn Rössel Waugh.*

A Des Moines, Iowa, native with a background in art and photography, Nan Wright made her first teddy bear as a Christmas gift for her daughter and turned hobby into business in 1978 after the birth of her second child. Nan is a founding member of the Iowa Teddy Bear Makers' Guild and is its unofficial photographer.

    She is perhaps best known for large open-mouth bears with hand-sewn leather tongues, claws, and paws, and has won two Golden Teddy awards for her designs, which are made from imported synthetics, sometimes mohair, and have leather paw pads, one of which is branded "Nanc" with a branding iron.

"I guess I have a backwards way of creating new bears," she says. "I usually start with a name and make the bear to fit."

Except for an annual Christmas edition, most of Nan's bears, which range in size from 10 to 36 inches, are undressed. She does all of the work herself, completing 200 to 300 bears a year. Most editions are unlimited; limited editions run 75 bears or less.

They may be found in a few select shops or ordered by mail.

Value: Nan Wright bears range in price from $65 to $300.

LARA-ZANO

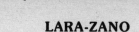

"The Little Orphan" by Lara-Zano is 20 inches tall, made of upholstery fabric, dressed in wools, and stuffed with polyester. He holds a fake fur dog. *Photo by Julie-Lara.*

Lara-Zano's bears evolved from her cloth dollmaking in 1975, and her approach to bearmaking speaks with a dollmaker's vocabulary.

Her bears, most of which carry a favorite toy or animal, are almost all dressed as small children. Sometimes these child bears play the parts of firemen, soldiers, or doctors, but it is evident they are children at play who just happen to be bears.

These charming creatures fashioned from upholstery fabrics, and dressed in wools and calicoes, are untraditional teddies, perhaps more doll than bear, and are readily identifiable by their inspired original whimsy. Most are one of a kind.

They range in size from 4 to 20 inches tall and are completely made by Lara, who completes up to 500 teddies a year. They are available through the mail or at shops.

Value: Lara-Zano teddies range in price from $60 to $300.

Appendixes

Addresses of Bearmakers
in This Guide

Please include a self-addressed stamped envelope when writing to the bearmakers listed below.

Durae Allen
7094 Ridge Road
Hanover, MD 21076

Maggie Anderson
Navron House
Route 25
Glen Cliff, NH 03238

Celia Baham
Celia's Teddies
1562 San Joaquin Avenue
San Jose, CA 95118

Linda Beckman
6143 Sugarloaf Drive
Grand Blanc, MI 48439

Jo-Ann Blair-Adams
105 Blair Street
Troy, NC 27371

Sandy Brazil
1743 Princeton Avenue
St. Paul, MN 55105

Regina Brock
2621 Brady Lake Road
Ravenna, OH 44266

Lynda H. Buckner
265 Dominica Circle W.
Niceville, FL 32578

Jane Carlson
139 W. Pershing Avenue
Phoenix, AZ 85029

Carol Cavallaro
162 Nortontown Road
Madison, CT 06443

Janie Comito
11532 First N.W.
Seattle, WA 98177

Barbara Conley
792 South Third Street
San Jose, CA 95112

Nancy Crowe
2400 Woodview Drive
Lansing, MI 48911

Suzanne De Pee
2208 South Valley Drive
Visalia, CA 93277

Brenda Dewey
RD 2, Box 863
Brimfield Street
Clinton, NY 13323

Holly Dyer
203 S. Water Street
Mt. Blanchard, OH 45867

Patricia S. Fici
418 Revere Drive
Monroeville, PA 15146

Sue Ellen Foskey
Route 1, Box 68
Ocean View, DE 19970

Gloria J. Franks
Goose Creek Farm
Pullman, WV 26421

The Rev. Chester D. Freeman, Jr.
398 S. Main Street
Geneva, NY 14456

Elaine Fujita-Gamble
9510 232nd S.W.
Edmonds, WA 98026

Diane Gard
1005 West Oak Street
Fort Collins, CO 80521

Dolores Grosseck
443 Militia Hill
Southampton, PA 18966

Mary Haggard
1034 Helen Avenue
Terre Haute, IN 47802

Billee Henderson
9312 Santayana Drive
Fairfax, VA 22031

Dee Hockenberry
14191 Bacon Road
Albion, NY 14411

Donna Hodges
P.O. Box 959
La Jolla, CA 92038

Mary Holstad
17831 145th Avenue, S.E.
Renton, WA 98058

Hillary Hulen
7804 Wagner Creek Road
Talent, OR 97540

Maggie Iacono
2 Raymond Circle
Downingtown, PA 19335

Charlotte Joynt
4817 Dakota Drive
W. Des Moines, IA 50265

Debbie Kesling
8429 Lambert Drive
Lambertville, MI 48144

Jacque Kudner
1727 Maybrook Road
Jackson, MI 49203

Bev Miller Landstra
87505 Biggs Road
Veneta, OR 97487

Tammie Lawrence
707 Dakota
Holton, KS 66436

Althea Leistikow
1025 S.W. Taylor
Topeka, KS 66612

Wendy Lockwood
2644 Knabe Street
Carmichael, CA 95608

Lynn Lumley
1600 Airport Road #66
Carson City, NV 89701

Judi Maddigan
1060 Harlan Drive
San Jose, CA 95129

Cindy Martin
5720 E. Kaviland Avenue
Fresno, CA 93727

Barbara McConnell
944 West 9th Avenue
Escondido, CA 92025

Margory Hoya Novak
5454 Alta Monte Drive
Santa Rosa, CA 95404

Nona Pebworth
Route #8, Box 341
Huntsville, TX 77340

Sara Phillips
726 Longview Avenue
Westminster, MD 21157

Beverly Matteson Port
c/o Paul's Pharmacy
Sheridan Village
Bremerton, WA 98310

John Paul Port
c/o Emily's Cottage
Sheridan Village
Bremerton, WA 98310

Kimberlee Port
P.O. Box 85534
Seattle, WA 98145-1534

Cynthia Powell
1506 Antoinette Court
Oviedo, FL 32765

Janet Reeves
640 E. Wheeler Road
Midland, MI 48640

Betsy L. Reum
1303 Moores River Drive
Lansing, MI 48910

Gloria Rosenbaum
259 Beverly Way
Gardnerville, NV 89410

Kathy Sandusky
25629 Oak Street
Lomila, CA 90717

Laurie Sasaki
2221 Parker, Apt. F
Berkeley, CA 94704

Maria Schmidt
536 Sunset Boulevard S.W.
North Canton, OH 44720

Steve Schutt
Mr. Schutt's bears are available
from "The Owl and the
Pussycat," Ft. Myers, FL,
"Bears to Go" in San Francisco,
CA, and "My Friends and Me,"
Leesburg, VA.

Christine Shelters
47637 Pintail Lane
Squaw Valley, CA 93675

Marcia Sibol
Box 498
Bear, DE 19701

Barbara Sixby
3965 Duke Street
Livermore, CA 94558

Jan Small
3001 Clifford Drive
Harlingen, TX 78550

Linda Spiegel
14782 Moran Street
West Westminster, CA 92683

Kathleen Wallace
164 RD #B
Narvon, PA 17555

Carol-Lynn Rössel Waugh
5 Morrill Street
Winthrop, ME 04364

April Whitcomb-Gustafson
149 Main Street
Boylston, MA 01505

Bonnie Windell
19620 N. Highway 57
Evansville, IN 47711

Pamela Sue Wooley
5021 Stringtown Road
Evansville, IN 47711

Beverly Martin Wright
890 Patrol Road
Woodside, CA 90462

Nan Wright
509 Olinda Avenue
Des Moines, IA 50315

Lara-Zano
1618 Chemawa N.E.
Salem, OR 97303

Teddy Bear Organizations

Check teddy bear publications for listings of organizations in your area.

The Good Bears of the World
P.O. Box 8236
Honolulu, HI 96815

An international organization dedicated solely to the donation of teddy bears to people in distress; GBW sets up local "dens" to further its goals.

American Teddy Bear Artist Guild
Contact: Rowbear Lowman
Scotts Valley, CA 95066

This national organization for professionals and beginners alike offers networking and conventions.

The Iowa Teddy Bear Makers Guild
Contact: Charlotte Joynt, secretary
4817 Dakota Drive
W. Des Moines, IA 50265

Westchester Teddy Bear Club
Vincent A. Tannone, president
P.O. Box 329
Lake Peekskill, NY 10537

A Teddy Bear
Show Calendar

Below is a sampling of the many teddy bear conventions and events available to the "arctophile," listed according to the month in which they usually occur. Please check with show promoters for exact times and places. The shows we list have a national reputation. Since we cannot possibly list every teddy bear event, the best way to keep current is to subscribe to magazines such as *Teddy Bear Review* and *Teddy Bear and Friends*, which publish up-to-date show calendars and advertising.

❧❧ JANUARY ❧❧

San Diego, California
Linda Presents: Annual Teddy Bear &
  Antique Toy Show and Sale
Contact: Linda Mullins
P.O. Box 2327
Carlsbad, CA 92008

❧ MARCH ❧

Schaumberg, Illinois
Teddy Bear Convention and Show
Contact: ABC Unlimited Productions
1 Thornwood
Flossmoor, IL 60422

❧ APRIL ❧

Baltimore, Maryland
Teddy Bear and Buddies Spring
 Frolic
Contact: Donna Harrison & Co.
300 Chestnut Avenue, Suite 306
Baltimore, MD 21211

Baltimore, Maryland
Baltimore Bear Faire
Contact: ABC Productions
1 Thornwood
Flossmoor, IL 60422

San Jose, California
Northern California Teddy Bear
 Boosters Club Convention and
 Show
Contact: NCTBB Convention
4718 Meridian Avenue, Suite 401
San Jose, CA 95118

❧ JUNE ❧

Clarion, Iowa
Teddy Bear Homecoming in the
 Heartland (an all-artist event)
Contact: Teddy Bear Homecoming
 information
201 First Avenue, N.W.
Clarion, IA 50525

Houston, Texas
Heart of Texas Teddy Bear Show
 and Sale
Contact: Vickie Veale
2722 N. Logrun Circle
Woodlands, TX 77380

Hummelstown, Pennsylvania
Teddy Bear Festival
Contact: Nancy Early
(717) 566-6187 or
   (717) 566-2885

Philadelphia, Pennsylvania
America's Great Teddy Bear Rally
   at the Philadelphia Zoo
Contact: Arlene Kut, Director of
   Public Relations
Philadelphia Zoo
34th Street and Girard Avenue
Philadelphia, PA 19104

Philadelphia, Pennsylvania
LiBearty Weekend (an all-artist
   show, held simultaneously with
   Zoo Rally but at the Hilton
   Hotel)
Contact: Serena Cohen
6240 Madison Court
Bensalem, PA 19020

Toledo, Ohio
Festival of Steiff
Contact: Hobby Center Toys
7856 Hill Avenue
Holland, OH 43528

✸✸ JULY ✸✸

Bloomington, Minnesota
Teddy Tribune Convention and Sale
Contact: Barbara Wolters
254 W. Sidney
St. Paul, MN 55107-3494

❧ AUGUST ❧

Amherst, Massachusetts
Annual Teddy Bear Rally on the
   Common
Contact: Teddy Bear Rally
   Committee
Amherst Rotary Club
Box 542
Amherst, MA 01004
(413) 253-3450

San Diego, California
Teddy Bear, Doll, & Antique Toy
   Festival
Contact: Linda Mullins
P.O. Box 2327
Carlsbad, CA 92008

Washington, DC in 1990;
   site changes annually
   (see below)
American Teddy Bear Artist Guild
   Convention (its location parallels
   that of the United Federation of
   Doll Clubs' conventions; an all-
   artist show)
Contact: Rowbear Lowman
1550 Scotts Valley Drive
Scotts Valley, CA 75066

❧ SEPTEMBER ❧

Baltimore, Maryland
Magic of Teddy Bears Convention
   and Sale
Contact: Donna Harrison
3000 Chestnut Avenue, Suite 306
Baltimore, MD 21211

Seattle, Washington
Washington Teddy Bear Lovers
   Convention
Contact: Louise Berry
18823 75th Avenue W.
Lynnwood, WA 98036

❧ OCTOBER ❧

Clinton, New York
Teddy Bear Artist Convention and
   Sale
Contact: Brenda Dewey
R.D. 2, Box 863, Brimfield Street
Clinton, NY 13323

Toledo, Ohio
Doll and Teddy Bear Show:
   Tribute to Teddies
Contact: Hobby Center Toys
7856 Hill Avenue
Holland, OH 43528

❧ NOVEMBER ❧

San Diego, California
Teddy Bear, Doll, Quilt, & Craft Show & Sale
Contact: Linda Mullins
P.O. Box 2327
Carlsbad, CA 92008

❧ DECEMBER ❧

Orlando, Florida
Walt Disney World Teddy Bear Convention
Contact: Walt Disney World
P.O. Box 10,000
Lake Buena Vista, FL 32830-1000

Glossary

ADVERTISING BEARS. Specific advertiser's name is connected to or on the bear. Can be a product sold in stores or given away as premiums.

ALPACA. One type teddy bear plush woven mainly from the fine wool of a South American mammal, the "Lama Pacos," related to the Llama.

ANTIQUE BEAR. A bear made in a much earlier time period, having special value because of its age.

ARCHIVES. The accumulated body of records preserved by an organization or company from the past and the present for knowledgeable use in future times.

ARCTOARTISTE. Bear artist.

ARCTOPHILE. Bear lover (or collector).

ART BEAR. Creation in any media with the bear as subject matter, intended as an art form and made by a recognized artist.

ARTISAN. A technically skilled craftsman who many times makes bears designed by others; sometimes works with original artist, often under their direct supervision.

ARTIST ORIGINAL. The complete bear and accoutrements personally designed and handmade by a person recognized as an artist in the fullest emotive sense.

AUCTION TERMS.
  Absentee bid. Some auction houses allow advance bids by mail or telephone, if you are unable to attend the auction in person.
  Buyers premium. Additional charge levied by gallery on final bid to be paid by the buyer.
  Phone bid. To bid during an auction while on the telephone, instead of attending in person.
  Sealed bid. Bid unknown to all but auctioneer, until after all sealed bids are in; then opened.
  Seller's premium. Additional charge levied by the gallery to be paid by the seller on top of the commission paid to the auction house.
  Starting bid. Lowest bid the auctioneer begins with on a lot.
  Lot. Each item or sometimes a group of items is given a number to refer to during the auction and in auction catalog.

BEAR ARTIST. Skilled artist who uses original concepts in design and personally creates an art form using the bear as subject matter.

BEARMAKER. General term describing anyone at any skill level who makes a bear derived from any source.

BRUIN. A name used for the real bear. Also used for bear-shaped toys; usually the more wild appearing early mechanicals and the bear on all fours.

CELEBRITY BEAR. A bear identified with, named by, or for, a celebrity, who may or may not actually create the design for the bear.

CENTER-SEAM. In general, the seam traveling down the center of a bear's head, usually from the back of the neck to the nose tip.

CHARACTER BEAR. A bear who becomes more than ordinary due to distinguishing features, adventures or stories written about them such as Pooh, Rupert, Theodore B. Bear, Super Ted, Paddington, etc.

CIRCUS BEAR. Bruin-type bear standing upright with ring in the nose as in some early electric-eye bears. Any clown-type bear is also thought of as a circus bear.

COLLABORATION. Artist-designed, but handmade by persons assisting the creating artist or designer; in cutting, stuffing or dressing.

COMMEMORATIVE BEAR. Bear produced to bring attention to an important event or anniversary.

COMMERCIAL DESIGN. A design created specifically for production by a company or individual to sell to the public.

CONCEPT. An original thought process from which an artist structures or designs a brand-new artistic entity.

CONFORMATION. Body style and proportions.

COTTAGE INDUSTRY. Small-size manufacturer with some employees paid by the hour; others who work in their respective homes, paid "by the piece." Sometimes a cottage industry is a "family company" with owners and employees from the same family.

DESIGNER. Person who does original design work for self or company. Drawings or patterns may be the total involvement. May or may not produce prototypes.

DISPLAY BEAR (OR ANIMAL). Any size bear used in a setting for wholesale or retail display purposes. Some elaborate displays are mechanized for animation.

ECCENTRIC WHEELS. Wheels on animals that have offset axles so they go up and down, as well as forward and backward.

EXCELSIOR. Long, thin, wood shavings used for stuffing and packing. Steiff has used it since their earliest toys and still has workers skilled in its use for their limited edition bears today.

EYE TYPES.
   Shoe-button. Of papier-mâché, pressed leather, etc., have wire loops on backs for sewing on.
   Blown glass. A color with a black pupil or solid black. Have wire loops on back for sewing on or stickpin wire that pushes into eye area.
   Enameled or painted metal.
   Thread in stitches or "French knots."
   Celluloid or plastic rounds. With internal flat movable discs.

Googley eyes. Either painted to look to one side, or with a movable apparatus so that they actually do move back and fourth.
Plastic. Of various colors with black or dark brown iris.
Electric eye bulbs. In small metal sockets; wire connected internally to an off and on switch elsewhere in bear.

FAIR MARKET PRICE. Retail price an item sells for regularly.

FAKE. Unsigned, unlabeled copies of early bears made to look and smell old or antique—deliberately made by unscrupulous persons to deceive collectors for illegal purposes.

FLOPPY. Soft, cuddly; usually not disc jointed, but with arms, legs, tails, etc., sewn into seams.

FULLY JOINTED. Animal has jointed limbs with disc joints and head that turns, i.e., "swivel head."

GROWLER. Voice box inside bodies that emit growling or roaring sounds. Double growler found in some bears.

HANDMADE. Made and assembled by hand. May be machine sewn, hand finished, and assembled by one person, or many on an assembly line.

HANDSTITCHED. Completely sewn by hand; no machine work at all.

HUMP. Upper back of teddy bear's torso; curved out and rounded like the real hump on live bruins.

INNOVATION. Something brand new under the sun, with no antique or modern precedent.

JOINTS. Where an appendage is joined to the body. May have sewn joints; or internal discs joints of metal, wood, hardboard, pressed cardboard or plastic connected with cotter pins, rivets, nails, or plastic rods; or wire hooked into appendages, then pushed through the body; or nylon thread from appendages through body.

KAPOK. A silky fiber obtained from the fruit of the Malaysian silk-cotton tree and used for soft stuffing in teddy bears and toys from the early 1900s on. Used in combination with other stuffing such as excelsior.

LIFE SIZE. Very large, detailed bears and other animals. Some referred to as "studio size" pieces.

LOGO. Trademarks and advertising marks used on identifying labels, tags, buttons, medallions, etc., by the creating individual, company, or manufacturer. These may change through the years and new ones may then be used for identification of toys produced.

MADE-ON. Clothing or other accoutrements made as an unremovable part of bear or other toy.

MANUFACTURER. A company or individual owning or operating a factory within the U.S.A. or overseas, for mass production. May employ "in house" designers or "freelance" designers.

MASK-FACE. Cloth, rubber, vinyl, wood, or porcelain face inserted into, or sewn into, the plush head of the toy.

MINIATURE TEDDY BEAR. Small teddy bears of approximately 5 inches and under.

MINT CONDITION. In "unplayed with" condition; as if newly purchased.

MIXED MEDIA. When two or more differing materials are used together in the same art form.

MOHAIR. A type of plush made from the long silky hair of the Angora goat, often with a mixture of cotton and wool in the woven backing of the fabric.

MULTI-FACE. Two or more faces of differing types of expressions existing together on the same head.

ONE OF A KIND. One piece produced, only never to be produced again.

OPEN EDITION. Many pieces produced with no limit to the number ultimately created.

PAPIER-MÂCHÉ. A material made from paper pulp or shreds of paper mixed with glue or paste. Can be molded into various shapes. Used for some shoe-button eyes.

PROTOTYPE. First handmade model from an original design or pattern. Made to be used as a sample for further production.

PROVENANCE. The "life history" of a bear—where it has been and who has owned it. If connected with a famous person or an event of great significance, its value may be greatly enhanced.

PUBLIC DOMAIN. The status of products, processes, and publications that are not protected under patent or copyright.

RARE. Seldom, if ever, seen. Not common.

REPAIR. To mend or otherwise fix damage and injuries.

REPRODUCTION BEAR. Legitimate copies of an antique, modern, or original. Usually signed and labeled.

RESTORE. To bring back as close as possible to the previous or original condition with repair, cleaning, and careful reconstruction.

REXINE. Material resembling oilcloth used for paw and foot pads on many English teddy bears.

ROD BEAR. Early 1900s Steiff Teddy Bear, possibly a prototype, jointed by heavy metal rods instead of double disc joints. Rod extends from single disc inside hip, through body, to inside of opposite hip. Arms are attached in same general manner. Additional metal rod extends upward from arm rod into the base of the head and is secured there.

SQUEAKER. Squeeze boxes of various sizes and construction that emit a noise when pushed or depressed.

STATIONARY. In a fixed position; not movable.

TEDDY BEAR. Toy bear named after President Theodore Roosevelt. Not as ferocious appearing as the real bear or the early toy bruins.

TEDDY BEAR ARTIST. A person recognized as an artist who creates an original teddy bear; concept to design to patterns, entirely handmade.

TRADITIONAL. Passing down of customs from generation to generation. A precedent influencing the present.

TWILL. Type of heavy ribbed cloth sewn into the head as nose section, along with the center gusset.

URSINE. Of or characteristic of a bear.

WHOLESALE PRICE. Selling price to the retail market.

YES-NO. Bear or animal with mechanism manually operated that makes head nod up and down or turn back and forth.

ZOTTY-TYPE BEAR. Standing teddy bear, usually of frosted or tipped mohair with open mouth lined with felt and paws turned under.

Bibliography

BOOKS

Bialosky, Peggy and Alan, *The TeddyBear Catalog* (Workman, 1985).

Brooks, Jacki, *Teddy Bears on Parade Down Under* (Australian Doll Digest, 1986).

Bull, Peter, *The Teddy Bear Book* (Hobby House, 1986).

Cieslik, Jürgen and Marianne, *Button in Ear: The History of the Teddy Bear and His Friends* (Jülich/W. Germany, 1989).

Gottschalke, Elke, *Geliebte Steiffe-Tiere* (Laterna Magica, 1984).

Greene (Venturino), Joan, and Ted Menten, *Complete Book of Teddy Bears* (Publications International, 1989).*

Hebbs, Pam, *Collecting Teddy Bears* (William Collins and Sons, 1988).

Hutchings, Margaret, *Teddy Bears and How to Make Them* (Dover Books).

Maddigan, Judi, *Learn Bearmaking* (Open Chain Publishing, 1989).*

Mandel, Margaret Fox, *Teddy Bears and Steiff Animals* (2nd series) (Collector Books, 1987).

Menten, Ted, *The TeddyBear Lovers Companion* (Running Press, 1989).*

Mullins, Linda, *The Teddy Bear Men, Theodore Roosevelt and Clifford Berryman* (Hobby House, 1987).

——, *Teddy Bears Past and Present* (Hobby House, 1986).*

*Indicates books covering contemporary, handmade teddy bears.

Schoonmaker, Patricia N., *A Collector's History of the Teddy Bear* (Hobby House, 1981).

Volpp, Rosemary and Paul, Donna Harrison, and Dottie Ayres, *Teddy Bear Artist Annual* (Hobby House, 1989).*

Waugh, Carol-Lynn Rössel, *Teddy Bear Artists: Romance of Making and Collecting Teddy Bears* (Hobby House, 1984).*

MAGAZINES

Bear Tracks: The Magazine of the Good Bears of the World, P.O. Box 8236, Honolulu, HI 96815.

Collector's Showcase, 1018 Rosecrans Street, San Diego, CA 92106.

Teddy Bear and Friends, 900 Frederick Street, Cumberland, MD 21502.

Teddy Bear Review, Collector Communications Corp., 170 Fifth Avenue, New York, NY 10010.

The Teddy Tribune, 254 W. Sidney, St. Paul, MN 55107.

Index

DOLLS — ENCHANTING AND COLLECTIBLE!

The Official® Identification and Price Guide to Antique and Modern Dolls explores the fascinating world of dolls, from Dresden china faces and porcelain figurines to Victorian fashion dolls and contemporary cuddley babies.

This invaluable sourcebook, in a unique format, offers the most comprehensive information on doll collectibles!

✰ Over 500 photos...lavish eight-page color insert...fully indexed!